Is There a Psycho i.. ....

Kerry Daynes is a forensic psychologist. She runs her own private psychology practice and works with her team of psychologists and psychotherapists for a variety of agencies, including making contributions to major police investigations. An average week can involve working with everything from stressed-out parents to serial killers. She also acts as an expert witness in criminal and family court proceedings. She has worked with some of Britain's most complex criminals in prison and community settings. Kerry regularly makes expert comments for TV and radio, including appearing in the Sky series 'Killing Mum and Dad' and the Channel 4 'Mania' series. She presented 'The Making of a Monster' series for the Crime & Investigation Channel in 2008, examining the background of notorious killers.

Jessica Fellowes works as a freelance writer and journalist, writing for the *Mail on Sunday*, *Daily Telegraph*, *Sunday Times Style* and *Psychologies*. Formerly she was a Deputy Editor of *Country Life*.

Is There a Psycho in Your Life?

KERRY DAYNES AND
JESSICA FELLOWES

CORONET

First published in Great Britain in 2011 by Coronet
An imprint of Hodder & Stoughton
An Hachette UK company

This book was previously published as *The Devil You Know*

First published in paperback in 2012

2

A CIP catalogue record for this title is available from the British Library

ISBN 978 1 444 71428 9

Printed and bound by CPI Group (UK) Ltd, Croydon, CR0 4YY

Hodder & Stoughton policy is to use papers that are natural,
renewable and recyclable products and made from wood grown
in sustainable forests. The logging and manufacturing processes
are expected to conform to the environmental regulations
of the country of origin.

Hodder & Stoughton Ltd
338 Euston Road
London NW1 3BH

www.hodder.co.uk

This book is punctuated with examples, taken from real life incidents in which the authors have recognised certain features that appear somewhere on the scale of psychopathic behaviour (a scale on which most of us appear somewhere). These examples are put forward as case studies for the reader to practice what they have learned in each chapter, and to see if they can recognise the traits which brought the examples to the authors' attention.

The reader would be totally wrong to assume that an individual is a psychopath simply because they appear in one of these case studies, or are mentioned elsewhere in the book.

At the beginning of each chapter is a character study, drawn to illustrate a generic psychopath's typical behaviour in that role – they are not based on actual persons and any resemblance to such persons, living or dead, is purely coincidental. Where I use examples from media reports, anecdotes and published reports, even if someone has been labelled as a psychopath by others, I cannot be sure of the accuracy of this myself without extensive assessment. The consequences to an individual of being expertly assessed as a psychopath are serious and far-reaching. This book is for information purposes only and should not be treated as any sort of diagnostic tool.

Thank you to Nicola Ibison at James Grant for her inspiration whilst on the tube. To Rowan Lawton at PFD and Eugenie Furniss at William Morris. Thank you to Charlotte Hardman at Hodder & Stoughton for her patience and special thanks to baby George for making his deadline so efficiently.

CONTENTS

THE SCORPION AND THE FROG – A FABLE

On the banks of a stream, a scorpion and a frog meet. The scorpion wants to travel to the other side and asks the frog to carry him.

'But how do I know you won't sting me?' asks the wary frog.

'Of course I won't,' replies the scorpion. 'If I sting you, I die too.'

Satisfied, the frog agrees and the scorpion leaps on his back. Halfway across, the scorpion stings the frog, dooming them both.

'Why did you do that?' cries the dying frog.

'It's just in my nature,' replies the scorpion.

1

THE PSYCHO IN YOUR LIFE

'I had arranged to meet my date, to whom I'd been chatting online, at a coffee shop. When I got there, I saw four other girls on separate tables waiting for him. He turned up with five flowers and gave us all one each.'

'I opened the fridge this morning to find that yet again my flatmate had finished off all my cheese. And I know she did that after a screaming row last night because she borrowed yet another of my dresses without asking, returning it smelling of cigarette smoke and with filth on the hem. Not to mention that I've been chasing her for the last four months for her share of the gas bill.'

'I was hurt recently by my friend at work. When he started just a few weeks ago, the two of us bonded instantly and went out for lunch almost every day. But recently he's been ignoring my emails and has been leaving the building shortly before 1pm with the deputy manager, laughing and joking together. It's hard for me to understand – particularly as I spent ages writing up his report for that important presentation he had to do last week.'

'Last week I pulled my young child away from Tommy in the sandpit. He was found screaming as Tommy was calmly bashing a mouse with his toy tool set, before trying to see if its legs would pull off one by one. When I admonished little Tommy, he looked up at me blankly. 'Sorry,' came out of his mouth but the smirk was unmistakable. Later, when his mother asked him to explain, he innocently *said it's not true. 'It must have been him,' he said, and pointed to my whimpering toddler.'*

Sound familiar? I'll take a punt and bet that you've come close to at least one of these scenarios. At some point in your life, you will come across someone who displays the key characteristics of a psychopath. In fact, scientists estimate that between one and three per cent of the general population are psychopaths. So, if you have 100 Facebook friends, the chances are that at least one of them qualifies (unless all your friends were made in prison, in which case, fifteen per cent of them will).

That sounds frightening – and it can be. But psychologists have come to understand that there now exists such a thing as a 'continuum of psychopathy'. While at the top end of the scale there are psychopathic serial killers and at the lowest end there are ordinary 'angels', somewhere around the middle are people who may not break the law but are nonetheless extremely hurtful and damaging to those around them.

You may not realise it: in fact, the chances are that you won't. Psychopaths don't often walk around with a bloody knife in one hand and a severed head in the other. They're much – *much* – more subtle than that. The psycho in your life may be your boss, your teenage child, your blind date, your relation, your doctor or your lover.

The psycho in your life may be wearing a designer suit or a tracksuit. The psycho in your life may be a man but could also be a woman. They may be a high-flying big-earner or a mother of five, living off benefits. The psycho in your life may be outrageously good-looking or riddled with acne. They may have dropped out of school at fifteen or be a highly qualified professional graduate.

In fact, the only thing that psychopaths have in common is a cluster of emotional abnormalities and antisocial behaviours that can wreak havoc in families, organisations and entire communities. It is a condition that is resistant to treatment. Devoid of any empathy, they are out to get what they want and they don't care who gets in their way. They will charm, manipulate and trick their way into your wallet, your home – even your heart.

With all this in mind, it's curious how everyone loves a psychopath. Think of Jack Nicholson's creepy turn in *The Shining*, Glenn Close's bunny boiler in *Fatal Attraction*, Anthony Hopkins' cannibal Hannibal Lecter in *Silence of the Lambs* and Robert Carlyle's fight-loving Begbie in *Trainspotting*: all of them hit movies that have had huge audiences paying for the privilege of shivers down their spines. Thrillers that leave us (almost) too frightened to turn the page and soap opera plots that star serial killers prowling the cobbled back streets of Manchester are hugely popular. Newspapers are also quick to capitalise on the draw of real-life crime, with shock-horror headlines and lengthy analyses.

At some point in your life you'll probably have referred to a 'psycho ex' – most likely because he watched too much *Top Gear* or dumped you for someone uglier – but we don't really understand what the term means. Nor do we even consider the likelihood of actually coming into contact with a bona-fide psychopath.

This book will teach you about psychopaths: what makes them tick; what goes on in their mind and in their brain (literally); why they are like that and what we can do about it. You'll be left equipped to spot the warning signs of a potential psychopath – how they operate in different roles and environments – and the best ways to defend yourself.

While a psychologist will assess a psychopath according to strict and detailed diagnostic criteria, for the layman there are red flags that could let you know when a psycho is in your life. Although this book should not be treated as any sort of forensic tool in identifying someone as a psychopath, it can give you warnings based on the principles of psychology. Make no mistake: if there is a possible psycho in your life, you need to lose them quickly.

Whether you are dating, having a trying time as a parent, being bullied at work or bewildered by your so-called best friend, this book will help you identify the devil *you* know.

I'm a consultant forensic psychologist with my own private practice. With my team of forensic psychologists and psychotherapists, we work for a variety of social, health and criminal justice agencies who trust us to identify individuals who present a danger to themselves or others. I have treated mentally disordered offenders in medium-secure units, worked with inmates in maximum-security prisons and high-risk individuals living in the community and have undertaken case work for the Criminal and Family Law Courts. From shoplifters to serial abusers, it is all in a day's work. Along the way, I have worked with some of the country's most notorious psychopathic criminals. And I know just how manipulative, charming and clever some of them can be.

I interviewed one of the very first psychopaths I ever assessed in a maximum-security prison. I had had to walk through several thick steel doors to get to him. For my own safety, there were panic buttons installed in the interview room and a prison officer stationed outside. I had been asked to assess him as part of his application for parole – he was serving a life sentence for the murder of his grandmother, whom he had stabbed to death in an argument about just five pounds. Yet, any observer watching me walk into the room for the first interview could be forgiven for thinking that it was he who was interviewing me. He had arranged for other inmates to bring me cups of tea, and he had re-arranged the sparse furniture in the room to make it more comfortable. He brought with him a written agenda for what *he* thought it would be useful to discuss. This was the first red flag warning me of his psychopathic tendencies: it is fairly typical of psychopaths being interviewed that they want to impress and start with an insincere concern for your comfort during the interview. Not to mention their innate sense of superiority, which means that they tend to try to control an interview as if it were akin to a press conference or similar.

I had been through the client's files and was under no illusions as to the crimes he had committed. And yet given the ease with which he approached my initial questions and his obvious 'gift of the gab', I still found him pleasant and charming.

On that first day, he told me the story of his life – his version at any rate – with himself as the tragic hero. He told me how he had been physically attacked by his mother, cried every night for his absent father and had been a quiet, shy boy who struggled with his self-esteem. He was so convincing that I could have almost cried along with him. But his emotional displays shifted rapidly (another red flag) from dramatic lip-biting and tearful hair-pulling to telling the odd joke, enquiring if I needed a cigarette break or complimenting me on my nice teeth!

When I asked him about his offence, he told me that he had been living with his seventy-three-year-old grandmother when he lost his temper and stabbed her (no fewer than seventeen times) with 'the soft side' of a kitchen knife. He thought it was probably shock at this uncharacteristic outburst and her pre-existing poor health that did his poor old grandma in, rather than the injuries he inflicted (red flag number three).

He told me that he had since spent his time in prison soul-searching and wracked with guilt – but when I asked him to elaborate upon these terrible feelings of remorse, he was suddenly lost for words (red flag number four). He had not taken the opportunity to have any kind of therapy whilst incarcerated but had nevertheless concluded that he attacked his grandmother when her shouting triggered a post-traumatic episode. He had since 'forgiven' both his mother for the childhood beatings and his grandmother for unintentionally triggering memories of the abuse. And that was supposed to make me think that everything was now hunky-dory.

On the second day of interviews, I pointed out the clear discrepancies between his account of his life and information in the files. He was completely unfazed by the inconsistencies and claimed mysterious blackouts and gaps in his memory (red flag number five). He went on to conveniently 'remember' committing aggravated burglaries, various swindles and the odd 'boyish prank' – such as catching the neighbour's cats and torturing them (flag! flag!). He told me, with a wide grin, about nailing a bird's wings to a tree, as though it was an amusing teenage jape. It was only when he eventually noticed the look of horror on my face (as a junior psychologist I couldn't help but react) that he suddenly changed tack and commented that he couldn't believe he had done such a bad thing. I asked him why he thought it was a bad thing. His reply? Because he was convicted of an offence and fined £50 as a result.

On day three, he told me of his post-release plans, which involved various schemes including training as a psychologist or children's counsellor. He had been taking full advantage of the educational opportunities available to inmates – so much so, in fact, that a prison teaching assistant had been transferred to another jail after it emerged he had managed to convince her that he knew her home address and intimidate her into smuggling banned items for him. 'It was only a joke,' he commented, 'serves her right for being so gullible.'

He also let slip that he had swotted up for his assessment. It turned out that this meant he had read reports of other inmates who had been turned down for parole – in the hope of doing better – and had read a book on psychoanalysis. At the end he put his hand on my knee and asked: 'How did I do?'

Over the three days that I interviewed him, he had gradually begun to score highly on my personal, completely unscientific, 'hairs on the back of the neck' scale. He also scored highly on the more valid and conventional measures of psychopathy.

SO WHAT EXACTLY *IS* A PSYCHOPATH?

The word psychopath literally means 'diseased mind' but although they can develop temporary states of mental illness just like anybody else, psychopaths are not insane. They are fully aware of and in reasonable control of their behaviour. Their acts are all the more chilling as they are not easily explicable as the result of a temporary sickness, but are part of a cold and calculating indifference to others that lasts a lifetime.

Psychopaths are not mad; but they can be very, very bad.

As the human race has evolved, ever since we shed excess body hair and learned to walk upright there have been people who seem impervious to the normal rules or the feelings of those around them – just think of Atilla the Hun, Caligula and Hitler. It can be argued that our entire history has been shaped by a number of extreme psychopaths, but given that there was no measurement of psychopathy until the 1940s, it is difficult to prove. Before then, society simply condemned them as 'morally bankrupt' or plain evil.

The American psychiatrist Hervey Cleckley wrote the first

major work on psychopaths in 1941, *The Mask of Sanity*, and was the man who first brought the term into popular culture. The book was written to help detect and diagnose the elusive psychopath and was pioneering in its distinction of psychopaths from those with major mental disorders who are more clearly 'abnormal'. (As an interesting aside, he went on to be the psychiatrist who was asked to give evidence in the trial of the US serial killer Ted Bundy, convicted in 1978 of over thirty murders.) Cleckley interviewed psychiatric patients and found that some of them showed few, if any, outward signs of defect yet repeatedly and shamelessly engaged in destructive, trouble-making behaviour. Their attitudes towards others and the world at large revealed marked deficiencies in the very emotional repertoire that identifies us as human beings. Cleckley concluded that psychopaths are unique in their inability to 'understand the meaning of life as lived by ordinary people'.

These days, the international gold standard for the assessment and diagnosis of psychopathy is the Psychopathy Checklist-Revised (PCL-R), which was devised by Dr Robert Hare in 1991. The PCL-R is a heavily researched instrument that measures the extent to which a person demonstrates the twenty fundamental qualities of a psychopath. A PCL-R assessment is complex and has to be conducted by a specially trained and appropriately qualified psychologist. The scoring is based on extensive interviewing and examination of file information.

To score thirty or more out of a possible forty on the PCL-R is enough to formally earn the label 'psychopath'. A score of thirty-five to forty is enough to make even Hannibal Lecter think twice about asking that person to dinner. The PCL-R allows for a sliding scale of psychopathy and all but the most virtuous of us are likely to be on that scale somewhere. Your average criminal scores between nineteen and twenty-two. Fine upstanding citizen that I am, my own PCL-R score is four.

The following will give you an idea of how the scoring works:

HOW YOUR NEXT-DOOR NEIGHBOUR MIGHT SCORE ON A PSYCHOPATHY CHECKLIST

0   Always popping round with a tray of home-baked cupcakes

2   Always has one eye on your biscuit tin

5   Persistently parks in front of your driveway

7   You find yourself watering their plants even when they're *not* on holiday

10   Is having an affair with your partner

12   Your milk and Sunday papers are rarely found on your doorstep

15   Lets himself into your house to watch your TV/eat from your fridge/sleep in your bed . . . regardless of whether you are there or not

17   Friends refuse to visit you anymore: their car tyres were slashed last time

20   The timeshare they persuaded you to invest your life savings in goes bust

25   Your dog is found dead on the pavement

30   . . . Two weeks later, so is your cat

35   Your partner is found stabbed on the pavement

40   The missing bodies are under the patio

In practice, the PCL-R groups the defining characteristics of a psychopath under two broad themes: personality traits and deviant lifestyle (see page 13). To be a psychopath you have to have evidence of *both* the lifestyle and personality features, although different individuals will have them in varying combinations.

Behind the eyes of every psychopath lies an impoverished emotional world, but you have to look very hard to see it. Psychopaths are unable to experience any subtlety or depth of emotion; what feelings they do have tend to be nothing more than short-lived and primitive responses to their immediate wants and needs. Therefore they also have very sparse empathetic understanding of the feelings of those around them; they are indifferent to the rights or welfare of other people, viewing them as mere objects to be manipulated at whim. And yet the psychopathic personality is able to conceal their cold and predatory nature behind a colourful and captivating charm. Psychopaths quickly notice what other people respond to, becoming excellent mimics of normal emotion and practised deceivers. They are often confident, entertaining and plausible raconteurs, but their anecdotes won't stand up to close scrutiny. Their flattery is seductive but insincere. They can be fun to be around for a short while as their recklessness and impulsivity can be exciting ('Let's go party!') but their self-assurance can easily tip into a domineering arrogance and you really wouldn't want to be around them when things do not go their way. A psychopath feels entitled to have whatever they want, at whatever price, and is prone to uncontrolled and aggressive explosions when they are criticized or frustrated. Like the scorpion in the fable, it is their nature to use and damage those who allow it, even though they often inadvertently shoot themselves in the foot in the process. Not that their ego will ever allow them to admit it: a psychopath will blame everybody and everything – but never themselves – for their problems.

There are no typical class or social circumstances in which you might find a psychopath, but there are common themes to the way they choose to live. They are likely to have been described as 'the black sheep of the family' from the outset and will have gone on to a lifetime of non-conformity, breaking rules, commitments and hearts. A psychopath rarely worries about the future, preferring instead to expend their energy pursuing novelty and excitement. He or she will never lose sleep over an unpaid bill, a lost job or even an eviction notice; they are content to be parasitic and rely on others for financial support and anything else they can get. Unsurprisingly, their relationships with others will be strained and superficial. They have no sense of loyalty and will move on to the next gift horse as soon as the last one runs out. They are unlikely to follow through on any type of commitment, or to worry about the future. Sex is indiscriminate, trivial or simply another means to an end.

PSYCHOPATHY CHECKLIST ITEMS

Lifestyle factors:
Many short-term live-in relationships
Juvenile delinquency
Breaking legal conditions/parole
Criminal versatility
Need for stimulation/prone to boredom
Parasitic lifestyle
Promiscuous sexual behaviour
Early behavioural problems
Lack of realistic, long-term goals

Personality traits:
Glibness/superficial charm

13

Grandiose sense of self-worth
Pathological lying
Conning/manipulative
Lack of remorse or guilt
Shallow affect
Callous/lack of empathy
Poor behavioural controls
Impulsivity
Irresponsibility
Failure to accept responsibility for own actions

Features of psychopathy overlap with diagnostic criteria for various personality disorders. The personality items on the PCL-R particularly have a lot in common with Narcissistic Personality Disorder; psychopaths and narcissists can therefore be usefully thought of as close cousins. People with personality disorders approach life according to rigid, narrow and distorted perceptions of themselves, other people and situations. Narcissists, like many psychopaths, have a fantastical and exaggerated sense of their own self-importance; they will haughtily embellish their skills, accomplishments and contacts to the point of blatantly lying. They are, by definition, pre-occupied with daydreams of themselves as famous, wealthy and successful. Their all pervasive self-centredness results in an inability to identify with the feelings or needs of others, who are viewed as inferior and readily exploited. Like psychopaths, narcissists fly into uncontrolled rages if their self-perception is challenged. Despite the similarities however, people with Narcissistic Personality Disorder don't break the rules in quite the same way as psychos; they consider themselves rather above the law but are not as out-and-out or randomly antisocial. Whilst they are frequently envious and disparaging of others they are generally not as calculating in their nastiness. Some people refer to psychopathy as 'aggressive narcissism' to convey the similarities between the two conditions but also to highlight the darker, more brutal and deliberate side to the psychopath.

According to diagnostic criteria narcissm is indicated by five (or more) of the following:

1   Has a grandiose sense of self-importance by, for example: exaggerating achievements and talents; an expectation of being recognised as superior without commensurate achievements.

2   Is preoccupied with fantasies of unlimited success, power, brilliance, beauty or ideal love.

3   Has a belief that he or she is 'special' and unique and can only be understood by, or should associate with, other special or high-status people (or institutions).

4   Requires excessive admiration.

5   Has a sense of entitlement: unreasonable expectations of especially favourable treatment or automatic compliance with his or her expectations.

6   Is interpersonally exploitative, taking advantage of others to achieve his or her own ends.

7   Is lacking in empathy: unwilling to recognise or identify with the feelings and needs of others.

8   Is often envious of others or believes that others are envious of him or her.

9   Shows arrogant, haughty behaviours or attitudes.

Equally, lifestyle items in the PCL-R are closely associated with Antisocial Personality Disorder. The 'Diagnostic and Statistical Manual of Mental Disorders' describe people with this disorder as displaying recurrent aggressiveness, a failure to sustain employment or honour financial obligations, and a repeated and remorseless lack of respect for the law. The majority of the prison population could probably be accurately diagnosed as having an Antisocial Personality Disorder but that doesn't make them all psychopaths, as they would also have to demonstrate a heavy dose of the other interpersonal and emotionally deficient features of the condition.

In order to get a full-house on a psychopath bingo-card, a person would need to: show a criminal CV to rival the Kray twins; have started racking up the arrests at a tender age; and have stuck two fingers up to the restrictions placed on them by frustrated courts and probation services. But although a long list of convictions will certainly contribute to a high PCL-R score it isn't a necessity for attracting a diagnosis of 'psychopath'. Although such convictions will demonstrate clear evidence of over half of all the PCL-R items, these can be in any combination. Not all psychopaths are created equal and just because one or two features are not present, doesn't mean they don't fit the overall picture. (Just because you meet someone who, for example, leads a parasitic lifestyle but is otherwise unexceptional, it doesn't make them a psycho. They may just be a sponger.)

The psychological make-up that defines a psychopath naturally attracts them to, and uniquely equips them for, a life of crime. Hardly surprising then that psychopaths are at least fifteen times more likely to be found in prisons than in the general population. Psychopaths are of immense concern to those of us who work in the criminal justice system because they are responsible for committing both a higher number of crimes and a more extensive variety of crime than any other group.

They are more likely than non-psychopathic offenders to commit violent or other forms of aggressive or threatening offences. The nature of psychopathic violence is also different to that of your common-or-garden criminal; it is more cold-blooded, planned and predatory, motivated by social or financial profit as opposed to 'crimes of passion'. But, although breaking the law is a popular lifestyle choice amongst psychopaths, it is certainly not the only one.

There is a distinct group, sometimes referred to as 'successful' or 'sub-clinical' psychopaths, who haven't chosen the obvious criminal career path. Perhaps they are particularly intelligent or well educated, less haphazard than the typical psycho, have developed highly polished social skills and managed to insert themselves into an echelon of society where they are accepted and trusted – for example as a lawyer, stockbroker or even psychiatrist. Other psychopaths may operate on the boundaries of the law: their behaviour may not be illegal – not quite – but it is immoral and potentially devastating to those unfortunate enough to be involved with them. Others simply just haven't been caught yet and shrewdly manage to manipulate, bully and frighten their close family, friends, colleagues and associates into keeping quiet about their misdemeanours. These successful psychopaths are likely to score around the mid to late twenties on the PCL-R.

The psychopaths who are in and out of prison are easy to spot. But, as Cleckley pointed out, some psychopaths 'keep up a far better and more consistent outward appearance of being normal'. Consider for example, an associate of mine who moved into a flat on the day that a grotesquely mutilated body was found in the communal bin area. It turned out that she had bought the flat next door to a sadistic killer. All her neighbours were understandably horrified about what had been going on in their midst and doubtless had sleepless nights imagining the brutal scenes that had played out just yards from their doorsteps. Many of them commented that they had long suspected that the guy from block three 'had psycho written all over him'. Meanwhile, my acquaintance simply enjoyed lapping up the media attention, adopting a shell-shocked expression on cue and providing exaggerated soundbites to any passing television news crew she could find. Strangely, she made no comment about the tragedy for the victim, let alone a passing observation on what a terrible world we live in. In fact, the only thing she said in private was how irritating it was that the police investigation was slowing down her house move. Even worse, that there might be a potential fall in property prices for the area. Through discussion with the neighbours, she was able to discover the identity of the deceased and later attended the funeral, not to pay her respects but in order to take photographs of the coffin and distraught relatives that she later attempted to sell to a newspaper. As it turned out, no one was interested in the snaps but she breezily informed me that her day hadn't been wasted 'because at least the buffet was good'. Whatever the psychological state of the killer (and I suspect that his problems went beyond simple psychopathy), it seemed to me that a different, albeit less dangerous psychopath had moved in on the day that he had moved out.

It is this wolf in sheep's clothing that is most likely to be the psycho in *your* life and is the main focus of this book. If your boyfriend has just been given a life sentence for his eighty-ninth offence, head-butted his defence counsel and nicked your purse as he was being led away to the cells, you don't need a book to tell you what's wrong.

THE CURIOUS INCIDENT OF THE CAT IN THE WHEELIE BIN

In August 2010, Mary Bale was caught on CCTV surreptitiously throwing her neighbour's cat, Lola, into a wheelie bin. The furore it consequently sparked – the clip had millions of views on YouTube – generated headlines such as 'Is Mary Bale the Most Evil Woman in Britain?'

Despite the public outcry at this outrageous act, it took a while for the police to decide whether or not it was criminal (it was – she was subsequently prosecuted by the RSPCA and fined £250 plus costs after admitting animal cruelty.) Illegal or not, was the bizarre behaviour psychopathic? It was clearly impulsive – Bale said she 'suddenly thought it would be funny' to bin the poor creature – and lacking any empathy for Lola or her owners. She wasn't discovered until by chance the next morning, some fifteen hours later. Bale's initial response ('It was only a cat') was unrepentant and suggested a 'what is all the fuss about?' attitude. It was only later, after public vilification, that she apologised and said it was 'completely out of character'.

Of course, after just one suspect act it does not necessarily follow that an individual is a psychopath. Unless Mary Bale has a long history of similarly cruel and unnecessary deeds not captured on film, the truth is that she is fairly unremarkable. Her story is probably more interesting for the public response to it. For several weeks, Bale received death threats, people called for her to be sacked from her job and the public lined up on the internet to convey their fury and disgust. The whole curious incident illustrates that when individuals violate either the written or unwritten rules of moral conduct we do not cope well with it.

WOMEN INCLUDED

The American Psychiatric Association estimates that around three per cent of men in the general population are psychopaths and one per cent of women. Female psychopaths tend to score higher on the personality than the lifestyle items of the PCL-

R, so are more likely to be the 'successful' psychopaths who manage to slip under the radar. Although research on psychopaths is increasing rapidly, to date the majority of studies have been carried out with males, which is why throughout this book we have tended to refer to 'him' more frequently than 'her'.

CAN A PSYCHOPATH BE CURED?

Bluntly, no, there is no 'cure' for psychopathy and sufferers can be unresponsive to generic offender treatment programmes. If anything, psychologists have learned that traditional therapies can have the unwanted effect of making a psychopath a more effective manipulator of others (as they learn to say what others want to hear). Specific guidelines have been published for treating this group that focus on persuading psychopaths of the benefits of modifying their behaviour, and developing skills to make them more socially acceptable, rather than attempting to change their underlying personality structure. It will be a number of years before researchers are able to ascertain if this strategy is truly effective.

THE PSYCHOPATHIC BRAIN

Some people believe that psychopathy stems from a specific neurological disorder. Whereas research does not suggest that psychopaths are brain damaged as such, their brains do appear different to that of non-psychopaths. For example, neuro-imaging techniques have shown that when psychopaths are asked to complete tasks which require them to process emotive words, different parts of the brain are active than in normal control groups. 'Faulty wiring' in the paralimbic system (a group of interconnecting brain regions that are involved in self-control and emotional processing) may be particularly significant. The evidence regarding brain abnormalities in psychopaths have led some scientists and legal teams to argue that they are not 'bad' but 'disadvantaged' or even 'disabled' (and therefore that more allowances should be made for their wrongdoings). At the opposite end of the spectrum, others have used the theory that psychopathy is biological in origin to support even more controversial arguments for identifying and detaining individuals even if they haven't committed a crime.

THE DIFFERENCE BETWEEN A SOCIOPATH AND A PSYCHOPATH

Occasionally, you will hear people talk of 'sociopaths' as well as psychopaths but there is no real difference: the two terms are used interchangeably. Broadly speaking, sociopath is more of an Americanism, so a psychopath can become a sociopath when they cross the Atlantic.

The term sociopath came about for two reasons. Firstly, because some psychologists thought that 'psychopath' was too close to the word 'psychotic'. Say 'psycho' and most people automatically think of Norman Bates, the sinister motel owner in the Alfred Hitchcock film. The film has enduring appeal (who hasn't twitched a shower curtain nervously?) and the director's manipulation somehow made a man in a grey wig and a granny dress scary. But poor, misunderstood Norm was mentally ill – the film's title (based on the book of the same name) actually refers to his being psychotic, *not* psychopathic. Psychotics act under the influence of delusions and hallucinations. Norman was probably suffering from a dissociative identity disorder and was in obvious torment ('Oh mother . . . God, noooo mother'). Psychopaths don't have distorted perceptions of reality and rarely have internal conflicts about the way they treat others, let alone a crisis of conscience.

Secondly, some social psychologists are convinced that psychopaths are created by both the family environment and an increasingly psychopathic society. They feel that the word sociopath emphasises both their beliefs about the origins of the condition and the fact that the associated features are damaging to entire groups.

2

IS YOUR COLLEAGUE A PSYCHOPATH?

At the desk next to you could be sitting a psychopathic colleague. They might be pilfering from your wallet, hacking into your computer or badmouthing you to the boss. Or they could be taking you out for lunch every day, telling you what a great friend you are and commending your latest presentation. Either way, they're hoping to use you to their advantage. A psychopathic colleague is not a team player. They look around the company and assess who will be useful to them. If they befriend you, it's because they've spotted a value that extends the reach of their pay cheque.

If you work with someone like this, you need to keep your distance. They depend on the malleability of others to help them carefully stage-manage their advance up the career ladder. And there are a few psychopaths on those rungs. Experts in psychopathy estimate that, aside from the criminal population, psychopaths are more frequently found in the corporate world than anywhere else.

I used to work for a small architectural practice in Glasgow. There were just five of us senior designers, including the husband and wife team, Sam and Ella, who owned it. Plus an assortment of interns, junior designers and an office assistant. Although the practice was small, we had a good reputation and were really pretty successful, always with a lot of contracts on the go. Because we did project management of builds, we would be handling quite large sums of money on behalf of our clients. Several hundred thousand pounds would pass through the company bank account: paying builders, interior designers, building suppliers and so on. Our fees were the least of it.

As the practice grew, Sam and Ella sometimes found it hard to keep up with all the admin, particularly as they were busy themselves with their own commissions. But, luckily, we had a brilliant office assistant called Judy. Judy was in her forties and quite mumsy-looking. That's probably partly why we loved her – compared to all the trendy, hard-nosed city people we worked with, she was very cosy. She was one of those people who was always there when you needed her with a sympathetic ear and a constant supply of biscuits in the tin when you needed one. She worked quite long hours – we all did – and you could rely on her to think of things to keep up morale. Like getting in a few bottles of beer so we could toast the end of the week.

She was also ruthlessly efficient. She hadn't been there long, a few months, before she'd overhauled all the book-keeping and instructed Sam and Ella to set up different bank accounts to make the handling of all the clients' money much easier. Sam was a bit hesitant at first – it's not as if Judy was a qualified accountant after all – but Ella insisted. After all, they had an accountant who did all the end-of-year tax stuff – they just needed to keep on top of their clients' money and if they had someone in house, whom they totally trusted, then that was the best solution.

Having Judy look after it all just took the pressure off. And clients loved her too – they soon learnt that it was quicker and easier just to call Judy to let her know what money would be coming through, than to bother Sam or Ella with it. Suppliers, too, preferred to talk directly with Judy as she would always know what was what and could sort out their demands quickly. Every week, Judy was supposed to have a catch-up meeting with Sam and Ella and go over all the week's transactions and demands, but this soon got lost in the Friday night beer session. But Ella would make sure that at least once a month she'd have a good chat with Judy. The trouble was, they would start to go over work matters but they often got sidetracked.

Then small things started to niggle at us. One time, when Sam and Ella were away, Judy came to me and asked me to sign a form that would authorise her to sign off all expenses – without a company co-director having to see it. She said that Sam and Ella had agreed to it, just forgotten to sort it out before they went on their holiday. I said that I couldn't sign it but would be happy to have a meeting to discuss it with her and Sam or Ella when they got back. She just said 'of course' and went off. It was only when she was arrested a few weeks later that I remembered she'd never arranged that meeting.

Then a couple of suppliers started calling Sam and Ella, claiming they hadn't been paid, when Judy said they had. At first, we just put it down to some sort of banking error. But when a client called and said that Judy had called her at home asking her to pay the money for building materials two weeks earlier than expected, alarm bells went off. Sam and Ella spent a weekend going through the books and the bank statements and to their horror realised that Judy had been skimming money off the accounts for two years – £500 here, a couple of thousand there. It all added up to tens of thousands of pounds. When Judy's case went to court, we discovered that she had started her swindles just two weeks into the job. We'd all been well and truly had.

Jake, architect and psychopath victim

Judy is a classic workplace psychopath. Which might seem odd at first – she doesn't fit the city-slicker stereotype that you might expect. She's not a man, for a start. She was mumsy, rather than smartly turned out in a well-cut suit. The firm she worked at was small, rather than a large, anonymous corporation where it is easier for someone up to no good to hide. And it's true that the erudite, shrewd psychopath is most likely to choose a larger company to enact his games. Psychopaths of this kind are selectively work-shy – they don't see why they should be lifting a finger to do anything that doesn't directly benefit them when there's someone else around to do it for them. A great many are drawn to the larger organisations where there is greater scope for impressive promotions and job titles – bringing power and money – and there are more subordinates available for manipulation and abuse.

> There are more narcissists in the business world than in the criminal population. Hare has remarked that if he couldn't have studied psychopaths in a prison setting, he would have done his research on stockbrokers or telemarketers.[1]

But Judy was a clever psychopath. She used her mumsiness to her advantage – taking a job in a small practice where cosiness was practically a prerequisite. Using her warmest voice and winning smile, she had only to pull the wool over her bosses' eyes and the rest of the firm followed. Her biscuit tin and empathetic act – make no mistake, it was an act – prevented anyone from watching her do her job too closely. She knew, in other words, that she was the last person anyone would suspect.

Furthermore, Judy was working alone. The fact that she was a department all of her own, with no one monitoring her daily schedule, was just perfect. Judy, it seems, displayed the classic characteristics of a working psychopath as outlined by Paul Babiak and Robert Hare in their book, *Snakes in Suits: When Psychopaths Go To Work*. Less aimless and more controlled than the prototypic psychopath, an employed psychopath will seek three targets out in order to achieve their own, cruel, ends: the Pawns, Patrons and Patsies.

'Pawns' are the people who have something that the psychopath wants. In Judy's case, these were the clients and Jake, for his helpful signature. But it's not always the person who has the keys to the safe that is the psychopath's pawn. A PA with access to the CEO's diary and address book is a good target. Or the known office gossip, who can spread the 'good' word about the psychopath so that people believe their reputation and don't look any deeper, all the while feeding him with information he needs. ('If you get Jane on the red wine, she'll tell you anything.' 'Word is that Bob's in the firing line – one more mistake and he's out.') Or an IT worker who finds himself befriended and after drinks down the pub one Friday after work he's asked for help to hack into the boss's emails. ('It's fine – I just need to sort something out for him and he'll kill me if he comes in on Monday and I haven't done it – help a mate out, eh?')

'Patrons' are those who are in a position of power. In Judy's case it was Sam and Ella. Not just because they were the company bosses, but because they were the ones who would act as cheerleaders for Judy. If Sam and Ella said she was OK, then as far as everyone else was concerned – colleagues, clients and suppliers – she was. A patron in a larger, corporate work setting could be the middle manager who recommends the psychopath for a pay rise. Or the HR manager who recommends him for a promotion.

'Patsies' are mere cannon fodder for the psychopath. They are the people office psychopaths will step on to make their way to the top, bet that Judy had identified those less than organised suppliers to point the finger at in the wake of any seeming financial 'blunder'. If something goes wrong, the patsies are always the ones to get the blame. They might be the downtrodden under-manager endlessly devising systems that never get off the ground, or the person who never makes that promotion and is the butt of every joke or prank (stapler in jelly, anyone?).

THE SEVEN SIGNS OF THE PSYCHOPATHIC COLLEAGUE

He could be at the desk next to you. Unless you have a pretty low view of your bosses, you'll have assumed that as he got the position he must have some solid credentials: a certain level of education, a keen knowledge of the field, previous relevant experience and a decent reference or two.

Sign I A psychopath actually finds it easier to target top jobs where the key words on the job spec are vague things such as 'leadership' and 'people management' rather than any hard and fast qualifications. Their CV will focus on more general personal qualities, which are easier to embellish and harder to quantify. With a persuasive charm as their weapon, the job is theirs. Less than ten per cent of communication is the spoken word and psychopaths know that it is not necessarily what they say, but how they say it, that is important. They manage to impress in a job interview with little more than a reassuringly firm hand-shake and the charismatic confidence and authority with which they trot out all the current buzz-words, but actually they say little of any real substance. Once they have their foot in the door, they are rarely questioned; colleagues naturally assume that if someone has got through the hiring process then they must be competent.

The culture that surrounds us can suppress or encourage the development of certain aspects of personality.[2] Generally speaking, psychopaths in the UK are very similar to the ones in the US but American psychopaths tend to score higher on the PCL-R items that measure arrogance and charm.[3] In a direct comparison between Scottish psychopaths and North American psychopaths, it was found that the Scottish displayed an overall lesser degree of psychopathic traits.[4] But this doesn't mean that a psycho from the Highlands is vastly different to his non-kilt-wearing peers; it is simply that the glib, charming and superficial manners are missing. After all, no Scot ever told you to have a nice day!

When your new colleague first arrived, perhaps your boss asked you to show the starry new addition to the team around. Naturally, you will have felt pleased to be picked out in this way. So it was a bonus when the newbie seemed keen to befriend you – he obviously thought you were someone to be reckoned with in the office and, as luck would have it, is passionate about the same football teams as you. You might decide to give this kindred spirit the benefit of your wisdom and not only help him find the stationery cupboard and the executive washroom but also fill him in on a few vital details. Such as who the most efficient typist is, the manager to take the slightly ropy expenses form to when you need it signed off and even Janey, the canteen server who always gives generous helpings.

Sign 2 Psychopaths are convincing and subtle flatterers. They'll quickly size you up and align themselves with you in order to check out your potential worth to them. They will deliberately reflect the interests of the person they are targeting to manipulate them into thinking that they really are friends. Those who have been conned by psychopaths have often been heard to say sadly afterwards: 'I thought I'd made a really good friend – we had so much in common.'

Even serial killers have to earn their crust with a day job

- Harold Shipman (doctor; thought to have killed about 250 people).

- Ted Bundy (lawyer who undertook his own defence in court and worked for a suicide prevention hotline; killed thirty-six young women).

- John Gacy (director of a successful company and part-time clown; murdered young gay men, burying them under his house).

- Steve Wright (Fork-lift truck driver; murdered five women and became known as the Ipswich Ripper).

- Gary Ridgeway (industrial truck painter; murdered at least forty-eight people).

- Dennis Nielsen (civil servant; murdered and dismembered seventeen men).

You have to be careful. Everyone has passwords on their computer (even if you haven't managed to get around to changing it from the standard PASSWORD1 given to you by IT). You don't leave your wallet on your desk or your handbag under the table when the fire drill goes off or if you go out for lunch. (You might, however, leave it if you nip to the loo or the canteen and certainly if you're just going to a meeting on the next floor.)

Sign 3 A psychopath will get a kick out of rifling through your desk or an unattended, unlocked computer for any clues as to weaknesses in your personality. There is none of the usual respect for privacy or personal boundaries in the psychopath's drive to assess your potential to them. A handbag, desk drawer, email account or even your text messages – nothing is sacrosanct.

Our new guy – let's call him Rob – has settled in quickly. But, to your chagrin, within a few weeks you realise he's no longer asking you to lunch but appears to be heading out the door with the firm's switchboard attendant several times a week instead.

Sign 4 Don't be surprised when you are suddenly overlooked for someone whom you just couldn't envisage that your co-worker would have been interested in. Corporate psychopaths will target not just the powerful but those with access to power. In this instance, Rob has spotted the switchboard attendant's 'pawn potential' and wants her to spill the beans on the boss's most important conversations and frequent callers.

(And it's not that you're gossiping but you can't help but notice that when he returns from lunch with the switchboard operator there's a rather dishevelled look about them . . .)

Sign 5 Seduction is just another means of gaining power for the psychopath and the 'no relationships at the office' rule won't even be considered. He considers sex with his subordinates as a perk of the job. Rob will be sleeping with the switchboard operator – but she will be just one notch of several on his bedpost that month.

Then, when the department manager is away, he takes it upon himself to chair the team meetings. He's soon name-dropping the chairman's name – Rob's been emailing him some complex ideas about how the company could embrace new technology. Looks as if Rob is in line for another promotion.

Sign 6 Psychopaths are stimulated by change and they are often good at adopting or at least seeming to adopt new technology – it makes them seem entrepreneurial and cutting edge. And the fact that no one understands these new gadgets and gizmos means they can talk convincingly without facing too many difficult questions. Not to mention that corporate psychopaths engineer to leave or change departments on a fairly regular basis – usually for a promotion, as they have impressed the people at the top so much in their current role. But also because they recognise the need to get out before all the people they have trodden on or misused are 'on to them' and get together. They know that they can only talk the talk – albeit loudly – without walking the walk for so long before being found out. By the time Rob's dazzling proposals to modernise his departments working practices have descended into chaos, he is enjoying his new, better paid promotion and it is his former manager who is left looking incompetent.

One day, the boss calls everyone in – there have been hard times recently, and you're all going to be asked to forego a pay rise this year. It's the only way that the company can survive. Bonuses are also going to be virtually non-existent and there are to be no more expenses claims. It's bad news – but you decide you just have to grin and bear it. It's not as if there are any other jobs out there and at least you still have a wage.

But to your surprise Rob takes it really badly. He storms into the boss's office and violent shouting is heard before he exits sharply. Your boss finally emerges, white-faced and trembling: he's not only suffered the indignity of the row but has also belatedly realised that Rob has been claiming vast expenses and persuaded the chairman to somehow authorise an early bonus a month ago. None of which will have helped the crippling losses the firm has been suffering. But it's too late. From that day, Rob is never seen or heard from again.

Sign 7 Psychopaths have no company ethic – they don't understand what you mean when you talk about working 'for the good of the company' and you will never hear them saying 'there is no "I" in team'. They just think that loyalty equals 'loser'. If they can't get what they want, or if they're beaten, they are simply, and often recklessly, out of there. Now that Rob is no longer able to claim huge expenses and a bonus he has no interest in staying in the job. If you're surprised that Rob has unwittingly revealed his skulduggery, don't be. Remember, psychopaths are impulsive creatures and, in any case, Rob now has lots of new material for his flashy CV.

Usually no one makes a fuss; they may even write Rob a fairly decent reference. After all, the chairman doesn't want to admit that he was taken in by his smooth charm and shiny patter. Leaving without another job to go to, it isn't long before Rob is back in the interview room impressing others with his confident jargon.

The international professional services firm PriceWaterhouse-Coopers (PWC) has carried out global economic crime surveys every two years since 2003, asking over 5,000 companies to report on fiscal fraud committed by employees. This gives a comprehensive picture of corporate crime on a worldwide scale. As a result, PWC have drawn up a list of recommendations for companies. They suggest that management are alert to any executive who:

- Engages in activities indicative of a lack of integrity
  (*frequent attendance at lap dancing clubs and putting large
  purchases of cocaine on the expense account would probably
  indicate a certain lack of integrity – yet we often hear of these*

forms of entertainment being common in large corporations or even being encouraged as part of business 'networking')

- Is prone to engage in speculative ventures or accept unusually high business risks *(and yet . . . the most profitable businesses are the ones that take the biggest risks. Look at hedge funds. They positively want people who will accept 'unusually high business risks')*

- Displays a poor attitude toward compliance with regulatory or legislative obligations *(although anyone too familiar with the policies and procedures handbook is likely to be labelled a 'jobsworth' or potential troublemaker)*

- Is evasive, uncooperative, or abusive of the audit team *(who was ever nice to the audit team?)*

- Lacks a proven track record *(unfortunately, it's hard to spot psychopaths this way – they are rarely stymied by something as simple as faking referees)*

While this is a useful checklist, it also demonstrates that some potentially problematic traits are positively handy when it comes to success in the corporate world. Probably not quite what PWC intended.

NICK LEESON – THE MAN WHO BROUGHT DOWN A BANK

Nick Leeson gained infamy – and a lengthy prison sentence – as the man who singlehandedly brought down Barings bank in 1995. The bank was declared insolvent after reaching losses of £827 million: double its trading capital. Not bad for a boy from Watford who started as a bank clerk for Coutts when he left school just ten years before.

In 1992, having been with Barings – HM The Queen's

bank – for just three years, Nick was appointed general manager of a new operation in futures markets on the Singapore International Monetary Exchange (SIMEX), where the bank had a seat on the board. But were there warning signs of what lay ahead which might, had they been heeded, had led the bank to act differently? According to Judith Rawnsley, in her book on the Leeson scandal, *Going For Broke,*[5] before going to Singapore, Nick had been denied a broker's City of London trading licence in the UK due to an inaccuracy in his application. When asked if he had any county court judgements against him, Nick said 'No'. But the Securities and Future Authority, which grants the licences, ran a routine check and found that he had an outstanding judgement of £2,426 against him on behalf of National Westminster Bank. Barings were told of this by the SFA but when Nick was sent to Singapore soon after, there was no mention of it when he applied for a licence in the Far East.

A small but potentially significant warning sign, in other words, that someone missed.

Nick quickly started to make unauthorized speculative trades that at first paid off – with £10 million in trade payouts, he accounted for a reported 10% of Barings' international profits that first year, earning himself a tidy £130,000 bonus on top of his £50,000 salary.

But it didn't last. Soon Nick was forced to use one of Barings' 'error accounts' (an account used to correct mistakes) to hide his losses. The losses grew and grew – £208 million by the end of 1994.

It was reported after Barings had collapsed that in October 1994, Nick had spent a night in jail for exposing his bottom to two women and that Barings helped to cover up the story, which was otherwise going to be reported in a gossip column in The International Financing Review.[6] The fact that they had to cover up criminal activity, however minor, of one of their employees should have put Barings on alert – at the very least, they should have watched him closely from then on.

Finally, in January 1995 Nick lost what was essentially a massive bet on the Japanese stock exchange. Fleeing, he left behind the out-of-control debts and a note that said, 'I'm sorry'. He was arrested after being on the run for a week and sentenced to six and a half years imprisonment in the Changi Prison, Singapore, serving three and a half years before being released early for health reasons.

Now, married to his second wife, Nick is CEO of a football club in Ireland, has published books about his time as a 'Rogue Trader' (one of which was made into a film starring Ewan McGregor) and is a regular on the after-dinner speaker circuit. You can even catch up with him on his website, where he admits he has 'capitalised on his experiences.'

Perhaps he is more self-aware than we know: in 2001 he began a psychology degree.

CAN YOU NOW SPOT THE PSYCHOPATH? AND COULD THEY WIN *THE APPRENTICE?*

Read each scenario and then score each potential new recruit to Lord Sugar's company according to whether you think they are:

0 = A college you would be happy to share a desk and a pint with

1 = Just looking out for number one

2 = A corporate psychopath if ever there was one

There are four contestants in the series, each of whom have been marked out as the 'ones to watch':

a) James Kendall. Good-looking and bright, James is always well turned out in a beautifully tailored suit. He has a cut-glass accent and an impeccable CV that includes a good degree, a ten-year stint at a reputable management consultancy and a rapid rise through the ranks.

b) Sarah Silversmith. Sarah has expensively blow-dried hair, immaculate suits that show off her small waist and a range of designer kick-ass, high-heel shoes. She has a first-class degree and has run her own business − a branding consultancy − sold last year for £1.2 million.

c) Dave Witchell. Floppy haired and baby-faced, Dave was the darling of the production crew before the first take. His suits are not shabby, exactly, but they never seem to be quite done up and he has long ruined their shape by constantly stuffing his hands in his pockets. Anyone standing by is always a willing audience for his stream of anecdotes, quirky trivia and stuttering flirtation. His CV? No one can quite remember what it said but it seemed pretty impressive at the time they read it.

d) Jane Goodall. Cheap pencil skirts and white shirts are Jane's uniform. Jane is pretty tight-lipped when it comes to talking about her personal life or her family. But she's worked her way through the ranks and was recently made Regional Sales Manager for her latest firm, just after she sent in her application to the BBC.

In the initial BBC interviews, each contestant was asked − 'Why should we pick you for this series?:
a) James said: 'Because I know I'm the best candidate the show has ever seen. And no one wants to win more than I do.'

0   1   2

b) Sarah said: 'Because I can take this show to the next level – Lord Sugar can learn from me too, with the success I've had so far.'

0   1   2

c) Dave said: 'Gosh. You probably shouldn't pick me. But I'm frightfully good at making tea.' (And then he winked at the researcher.)

0   1   2

d) Jane said: 'Because I've worked hard since I was 16 years old for an opportunity like this and I won't let it get away.'

0   1   2

Shortly before filming begins, the contestants are invited to meet Lord Sugar, Nick and Karen informally.

a) James marches straight up to Lord Sugar and attempts to engage him in a conversation about CEOs that they both know. Lord Sugar is unimpressed but is unable to escape James's grip.

0   1   2

b) Dave discovers that he and Nick's son went to the same school and that their mothers share the same first name. He tells Nick that he's always been an admirer; surely Nick should be profiting better from his appearances on The Apprentice, rather than Lord Sugar?

0   1   2

c) Sarah sidles up to Karen and asks if her lipstick is Mac Really Red, by any chance? It is – and they have a long conversation about beauty tips, which Karen thoroughly enjoys. Everyone else is always so serious with her.

0   1   2

d) Jane introduces herself to all the other contestants, makes a mental note of their names and tries to find out their key likes and dislikes. She's a bit abrupt in her manner though, not quite charming enough, and a couple of them deliberately mislead her.

0   I   2

On the first task, the contestants are told to buy fish from an early morning market and sell it at profit to restaurants. James is task leader of his team.

a) James immediately sets up a temporary 'office' back at the Apprentice house and sends Sarah and Jane off to the market. He then spends the rest of the task calling PRs to discuss how best to launch his new fish business.

0   I   2

b) Sarah takes charge at the market – she sends Jane off to check the prices on all the stalls, while she has coffee with the market's general manager.

0   I   2

c) Dave puts in one call to a posh, blonde chef he happens to know and tells Sarah to arrange the sale. Then he, James and Sarah go out for a long celebratory lunch.

0   I   2

d) Jane checks all the prices on the stall, buys the second-from-cheapest and sells them all as a job lot to Dave's contact (as Sarah has asked her to do).

0   I   2

In the boardroom, Lord Sugar has hauled in Dave, James, Sarah and Jane – all on the losing team. (It turns out the fish was of poor quality and the chef refused to complete the sale.)

a) James says: 'I was assured by everyone that there were no problems – I was working hard to get publicity for the deal. That restaurant has made a big mistake.'

0   1   2

b) Dave says: 'Gosh. After all, I lined up the sale – the others didn't have to do anything except check the fish was fresh. I really feel that I've been let down here.'

0   1   2

c) Sarah says: 'If it hadn't been for me, Jane wouldn't have even found the market in the first place let alone known what to do when she got there. Then Dave never told us that the sale hadn't gone through.'

0   1   2

d) Jane says: 'I was conned by the fishmonger.'

0   1   2

Halfway through the series, the contestants and crew have a night out. It's a chance to let off a bit of steam.

a) Sarah gets drunk, is heard bitching loudly in the ladies about the other girls and then forces her mobile number on the cameraman.

0   1   2

b) Dave gets Nick and the producer in the corner, plies them with whiskies and cigars and soon they are off to a casino betting the producer's BBC expenses on a poker game. When he drops the producer back home – too drunk to stand unaided – he makes a discreet pass at his wife.

0   1   2

c) Jane refuses to touch a drink and is back at the house by 10pm to get an early night and catch up on her sleep.

0   1   2

d) James orders in a gram of cocaine and has a quickie in the toilets with the pretty young researcher – Dave tipped him off earlier that she was easy.

0   1   2

At the end of the series, our 'heroes' are the finalists. Lord Sugar sums them up before making his decision.
a) 'James – you're a smart one. You look the part. You've charmed your way around and you've made some clever sales. But I think you're feeding me bull – and I don't like it.'

0   1   2

b) 'Sarah – you've got a way about you, no doubt about it. But you talk too much. I find it irritating. And you've done well outside – so I worry. Why are you doing this? You'd be mistaken if you think you can teach me anything, I may be an old dog but I know all the tricks.'

0   1   2

c) 'Dave – you're a popular guy. Nick here – he's fought for you even though I've seen you in this boardroom more times than I care to remember. But I trust Nick. So I'm going to trust you. You strike me as the sort of bloke that can live off his wits. In many ways, you remind me of me as a young man.'

0   1   2

d) 'Jane – you're a hard worker. You're keen to make something of yourself. I like that. You can talk too much sometimes, but you know what you're saying. Yeah. You're alright.'

0   1   2

DID YOU SPOT THE PSYCHOPATH?:

DAVE is our psychopath here. He is the most slippery of our corporate snakes in the grass. Charming those who can help him and avoiding work whenever possible, his shabby suits and stutter belie his big ego.

JAMES is a potential low-level corporate psychopath – he's out for himself but with his thrill-seeking, reckless behaviour, he's self-sabotaging too.

SARAH could possibly score one or two points on the PCL-R – she might be willing to manipulate anyone she can manage to charm (but they are few and far between).

JANE is not psychopathic at all – she's just desperate to win and change her life but is only likely to have a career as the hard-working but unpopular office scapegoat.

SUMMARY AND ADVICE

The psychopath at work is a cunning beast. He knows that his new colleagues will assume that he's a normal, everyday bloke with the right qualifications for the job. Using this to his advantage, he'll shake your hand, while stabbing you in the back. Unwittingly, you'll be his willing pawn – fetching him the information he needs in exchange for basking in his high-achiever's glow. Stepping on the patsies as he marches to the top, he'll be sneaking into the boss's office, if not his shoes. The patrons in his game might be clever enough to have got to the top – but they're not so clever that they can't be fooled too. What's more, even if they eventually realise it, many won't be willing to let on they've been had. And the psychopath will simply move on to the next victim.

If you've read carefully, you'll know the warning signs. But what can you do about it?

- First and foremost, do not label your colleague a psychopath. That in itself could amount to workplace bullying and will not help matters. Instead, concentrate on building and keeping strong relationships with your other workers so that it is harder for the psychopath to intervene or manipulate you.

- Ensure that you know your company's policies and practices and check your options if you need to complain about someone. Be certain you save complaints for the important things though, as they'll be given more attention that way.

- Be transparent in your working practice – always tell the relevant people what you are doing and keep copies of all documents, minutes of meetings etc (this saves you from being the 'fall guy' if something goes wrong).

- Forget the law of reciprocity which says that if someone says or does something nice to you then you have to return the favour. Clever psychopaths know this and use it to their advantage. If a psychopathic workmate gives you confidential information or a titbit of gossip, a tip-off, or just a bit of seemingly sensitive personal information, smile sweetly but don't feel you owe them anything in return.

- Stay away from office tittle-tattle. Make your own assessments based on your own experience of people.

- If you think a team member is an all mouth but no action type, pin them down to discreet action or outcome points (rather than corporate-speak that doesn't actually mean anything). Then document and later review.

3

IS YOUR BOSS A PSYCHOPATH?

The psychopathic boss is probably one of the most dangerous psychopaths there are. Not just because of any crimes they may commit but because it is in this role that they are most heavily disguised: many of the psychopath's core characteristics are shared by a non-psychopathic successful business leader. In fact, we admire some of these traits as necessary to succeed in the arena of business, yet advise caution if we spot them in anyone else.

The psychopathic boss may be the CEO of a large corporation, dictating the company's ethics and responsibility to its shareholders. Or he may be a self-made millionaire, with a large personal staff. In either case, the consequence of this particular psychopath's actions will have a wide reach: whether it's the company that pollutes the environment through dishonest policies or lies to its shareholders or fails to honour contracts to employees.

If you find yourself working for a psychopathic boss you are probably working for a very successful corporation but the risks will be high. There may be some extraordinary rewards in the short term, particularly for those working in the finance sector, as the psychopathic boss will take big gambles that could pay off. But you would be wise to avoid putting all your financial security in your boss's hands.

Working for David Winner was a privilege. I couldn't believe my luck when I landed a job at his Winner Takes All company. He'd started with a tiny business thirty-five years ago, importing rugs from Morocco and selling them to big hotels in London – he was only nineteen years old. Eventually, that led him to buying a hotel, which he turned into a five-star success and from there he's developed an international chain. He also bought out a small media company and now runs, or has major stakes in, several TV channels, three magazines and a newspaper. He owns several properties here and abroad and his company has high-profile sponsorship deals. The WTA brand has the Midas touch – whatever he takes on turns to gold. And you should see his latest wife – half his age and absolutely gorgeous.

I was hired to work in his office – just as a gofer boy to start with. I was so excited. I was in charge of making sure he had his coffee in the morning, just how he liked it. He'd change his mind sometimes and be angry if I'd not realised that today it was the mocha skinny latte and not the double shot cappuccino but I didn't mind. You can't expect someone like him, a self-made billionaire with thousands of employees and huge business deals going down every day, always to be polite. It could be embarrassing in front of people but at other times he would be amazing. Once I was in a meeting with him and he just pointed at me and said to the others, 'See this bright spark here? I'm going to give him a car as a bonus. That's how well we're doing.' And he ordered me to go out and buy myself a little sports car. Of course, I couldn't – I don't even have a credit card and then he forgot about it later. I didn't like to remind him but it showed how generous he could be, didn't it? So it was a big shock when we found out he'd been using all the money from the pension funds to pay for everything. I'm OK, I'm still young. But I feel pretty bad for the old guys who have nothing left to see them through to old age. It's not been a waste though – I studied him. And I'm going to be as big a success as him one day. I've started selling carpets already.

John, 22, former employee

From my first day with David Winner, he told me to call him 'Dave'. I was hired as his PA and I'd been warned by the agency that sent me that he'd had seven PAs work for him in the last two years but I found him charming from the start. His diary was absolutely packed but every week he'd find time to take me out for a drink round the corner and make sure I was OK. We'd have a little gossip about everyone in the office because when you're the PA people often come in and moan to you about the boss but my loyalty was always to Dave. Then, one night, at the end of the week, he locked his office door and brought out a bottle of champagne. Somehow he'd heard that my boyfriend and I had split up and he turned on the sympathy. It wasn't long before I was crying on his shoulder and then before I knew it we were having sex.

On the Monday morning we were both completely professional with each other but it became a regular occurrence. He would never contact me outside the office but somehow I didn't mind. He knew how to make up for it – there would be little presents waiting for me now and again. In return I was very discreet and of course never said anything to his wife when she called. I probably got a kick out of it, to be honest. I know Dave did. Once, when he knew his wife was on the phone to me he put his hand down my shirt and kept it there when I passed on the call to him. Then one day I was in the ladies' loo and a girl was in there crying. She worked in the marketing department and she had found out she was pregnant. I was comforting her and she told me not to tell anyone else but that it was Dave's baby and he'd told her to just get rid of it. She didn't know what to do. I was devastated. Obviously I wasn't anything special at all. The next day, I resigned. I never heard from him again.

Jane, former PA

Dave and I were at school together and I'm married now to his sister. He used to tease me for being the swot but I got my accountancy diploma and then I went to work for him. Right from my first day,

Dave explained that my job was to make sure he was making money. I got very good at finding tax loopholes. Everything was strictly legit as far as I was concerned but sometimes, if a deal was worth millions, he'd say it was too much for me and he would finesse the details himself. He had several bank accounts, one in Switzerland, and different 'business partners' would be named as directors. As I said, none of it was illegal, but it's amazing what you can keep off the record if you know what to do. I know it looks shocking – what he did with the pension funds – but he was only borrowing money from himself to get new deals done. Those deals were going to make him a shed-load more money and then he'd have paid it all back. It was just bad luck that the last deal didn't work out – who could know that a Russian vodka company could go bankrupt? Dave's a good bloke. He didn't mean for all his staff to get let down. He feels terrible about it. He says that when he gets out of prison, he'll contact each one personally to say sorry.

Keith, accounts director and brother-in-law

Most of us spend our daily toil clocking in the hours, diligently hoping that keeping our head down, meeting our targets and keeping on-side with our colleagues will keep our jobs safe, or even earn us a promotion or two with a little extra for us on the payroll. We pay for our cars with payment plans and keep a close eye on our mortgages. The nearest we get to owning a private jet to fly to our own private island is when we buy a Lottery ticket.

Occasionally, we hope our dreams will come true – perhaps we'll write a best-selling novel or a distant relative will leave us a fortune. But in our hearts we know the truth: the people who earn the great fat wedges, live in mansions and splash their cash in tsunami proportions are those who take the big risks.

The multi-millionaires like Sir Richard Branson, Donald Trump, Bernie Ecclestone, Bill Gates and our anti-hero above, 'Dave Winner', didn't get to where they are by obeying orders and taking no for an answer. They got there through daring, cunning, ruthless ambition and imagination. These are men who dreamt of building empires – and then did it.

None of the above is a psychopath (except for Dave), but it is interesting to note how many successful entrepreneurs have some traits in common with psychopaths. In fact, you don't even have to be a world-dominating billionaire in a skyscraper penthouse to share traits with a psychopath. Just being a senior manager will do.

COULD HAVING A PERSONALITY DISORDER HELP YOU CLIMB THE CORPORATE LADDER?

A study by Belinda Board and Katarina Fritzon of Surrey University[7] tested for any overlap between the personalities of business managers, psychiatric patients and hospitalised criminals (the psychopathic and the psychiatrically ill). They found that three of eleven personality disorders were more commonly found in managers than in disturbed criminals. Two of these disorders have a lot in common with psychopathy:

*   Histrionic personality disorder (characterised by constant attention-seeking, theatrical expressions of emotion and a need for excitement. Histrionic individuals tend to be highly flirtatious and manipulative; they are often identifiable by their dizzyingly changing moods and their dramatic, yet vague, style of speech).

*   Narcissistic Personality Disorder: grandiosity, self-focused, lack of empathy for others, exploitativeness and independence (see chapter 1).

The most fascinating thing about the most successful of our 'successful' psychopaths is that they are admired as much for their psychopathic traits as for their bank balances. What a psychologist would call a 'lack of conscience' could just as easily be described as 'the steely determination to win at all costs'. Think about it. Let's take a highly successful advertising executive – a creative director at a big firm. We'll call this one Hank Hudson.

Hank has just won a prestigious award for his latest advertising campaign and, consequently, he is the subject of a big profile piece for a national paper. Looking at some extracts, we can spot the potential psychopathic signs – but you have to look closely. The journalist clearly believes that Hank is the sum of his parts, each of which is a necessary requirement to becoming a vastly rich and successful man.

> Hank Hudson, 43, may be the creative director of Muck & Brass, with the long hours in the office that his success requires, but with his tremendous, forceful energy, he always makes sure he finds the time to indulge in his favourite hobby: heli-skiing. And not just any old heli-skiing but always off-piste, in undriven snow. His face lights up when he talks about the time he was dropped at night, alone, and it took three hours of skiing to find his way to the nearest chalet.

> Nor does he leave the thrill of extreme risk behind when he walks through the office doors. A colleague remembers the time Hank risked hundreds of thousands of pounds of Muck & Brass company money by booking a billboard in London's Piccadilly Circus and putting an ad on it to win a pitch. Amazingly,

Hank not only won the account but the client offered to pay for the space.

Sign 1 A psychopath needs stimulation. Perhaps it has something to do with their inability to experience the usual range of emotion but they need more extreme thrills than the rest of us to reach that critical threshold where they are really having fun. They are prone to severe boredom and if they have the money to fund it, extreme sports hold a great deal of appeal for them. The riskier the better. And business is just another type of sport, the thrill of the chase in business can be even more satisfying for the psychopath than the moment when the big deal actually pays off.

Hank always knew he was destined for great things. When he was just fifteen years old, he quit his first job as a carpet layer, telling his boss that he was going to set up a rival company. Within a year he had done it.

Sign 2 Without question, most of the world's self-made millionaires wouldn't have got to where they are without being outrageous dreamers. Quite often they might have been accused of reaching for unattainable heights. Who would have believed a young Sir Richard Branson if he told them he intended to own his own train line, airline and island? Or might have laughed at twenty-one-year-old student Alex Tew when he decided to become an almost instant millionaire by selling his website's pixels (the tiny dots that make up the computer screen) for one dollar a dot. He became a millionaire. The proposals of a budding entrepeneur unfettered by convention or limits, might be interpreted as evidence of 'unrealistic goals' by a psychologist completing a psychopathy checklist, but is viewed positively as 'blue sky thinking' in the business world.

'The simple truth of the matter is that I am the best creative director alive and Muck & Brass is the best advertising agency. The clients don't choose us – we choose them. If someone doesn't like the campaign I've designed for them, then I'm not interested in working with someone so close-minded. Yes, I've fired a client or two.' And with that, Hank laughs, leans back and lights his cigar. Such self-belief is a little hard to hear but without it he'd probably still be a junior account executive.

Sign 3 As we know, a sense of grandeur and infallibility is common among psychopaths but it is an essential character-istic when we are talking about this particular breed of busi-nessmen and women. The conviction with which a megalomaniac plies her wares can border on delusional, particularly if they are attempting to sell ice to Eskimos. But confidence is an extremely powerful tool. An unshakable self-belief may even-tually persuade even the most sceptical of Eskimos that it must have some solid foundation, and they need what you are selling! Next time you hear a young braggart, ask yourself: is he psycho-pathic or on the road to riches?

A former boss of Hank's recalls how he never seemed to crumble under pressure. Even when Hank was getting bawled out for having spent several thousand pounds of company money on 'entertaining' clients at a noto-rious lap-dancing club, Hank's face would remain impas-sive. A client screaming down the phone at Hank that an ad placement was completely wrong wouldn't even make him flinch. It's this cool in the line of fire that has kept Hank holding on to his current clients even in the teeth of a vicious recession.

Sign 4 What Hank's former boss sees as coolness, a psychologist would call an inability to experience any depth of emotion. Put simply – the reason Hank doesn't crumble or flinch is because he feels nothing. He doesn't even bat an eye.

> We all tend to blink defensively when we are startled. Laboratory experiments show that the startle responses of non-psychopaths are large when sudden noises interrupt them from viewing unpleasant or threatening images. On the other hand, psychopaths hardly flicker.[8]

Not that Hank's battle to the top hasn't left him without some scars. Despite his intense loyalty to some of his staff – Hank's PA has worked with him for fourteen years – others are mere bodies left on the field. One of Muck & Brass's directors, who prefers to remain anonymous, remembers a time when Hank's own brother was working for a rival ad agency and was deep in negotiations to land a contract with a huge soft-drinks company. Hank invited his brother to dinner, got him drunk and got him to admit that the drinks this company made were 'foul, cheap stuff – I won't drink it even when they pay me to'. He taped it. The following week, Hank had the account. The director admits this kind of behaviour is pretty despicable but also says: 'Without Hank's willingness to win at all costs, this company wouldn't be where it is today – the second biggest ad agency in the world.'

Sign 5 What the flatterer calls a 'willingness to win at all costs' the psychologist would term a 'lack of conscience'. You have heard the expression, 'He would sell his own granny ...' ? That is the attitude of your über-ambitious psychopath. They are not inhibited by guilt, remorse or shame. If a psychopath appears to be loyal to anyone it will only be because they know they are useful in the long run. Hank has had the same PA for fourteen years. He's nice to _her_ because he knows he needs someone watching his back.

> Hank's first direct boss at Muck & Brass tells the story of when he gave Hank his job – as a junior account executive. 'We shook hands and I told him I was looking forward to seeing him start work on Monday. But, I said, he'd have to have a meeting first thing with our HR Manager. "Oh, you mean Julie Peasgood," said Hank. Surprised, I said yes. Turns out Hank had applied for the job nine times. By the end, Julie was simply worn down and agreed to send him up for an interview with me. That guy just doesn't care about failing – he keeps on trying. That's why we've won most of our accounts – he keeps on knocking on their door no matter how many times they slam it in his face.'

Sign 6 Psychopaths are relentless in the face of adversity. But what looks like a stoic bravery or gritty immunity to failure is actually just an inability to learn from punishment and modify their behaviour accordingly.

PSYCHOPATHS DON'T LEARN THEIR LESSON

Hare and his students conducted a series of studies in the 1970s that have since become classics in psychopathy academia.[9] Hare had his subjects watch a timer count down; when it reached zero, they got a 'harmless but painful' electric shock, while an electrode taped to their fingers measured their perspiration levels. Normal people would begin to sweat as soon as the clock started, in anticipation of the shock they knew was coming. But psychopaths didn't perspire a drop. They appeared to 'tune out' the impending unpleasantness, appearing fearless. This can also translate into having no learned fear of failure or the consequences of falling flat on your face – helpful when you are setting up your fifty-third entrepreneurial enterprise. In other words, psychopaths have no need to face the fear – they just do it anyway.

On a visit to Hank's beautiful town house in the smartest part of the city, I wait for him in his library. As you might expect, the shelves are weighed down by highly collectable editions of luminous authors such as Dickens, Trollope and Proust. But nearer to his vast, mahogany desk (modelled on the one where George Washington hammered out the United States Constitution) is an array of books displaying a multitude of interests. A guide to bee-keeping sits next to one on collecting lithographs; there are several books on classic cars and then several on Greek mythology. Hank catches me looking at them. 'Ah, yes,' he says. 'I'm an autodidact, you see. And you never know when a random piece of knowledge can inspire an idea for a campaign.'

Sign 7 Hank's claim to being a self-taught man may be true but however impressive his library, his knowledge is likely to be rudimentary. Martha Stout in *The Sociopath Next Door* writes that: 'Sociopaths sometimes exhibit brief, intense enthusiasms – hobbies, projects, involvements with people – that are without commitment or follow-up. These interests appear to begin abruptly and for no reason, and to end the same way.' A psycho-boss may impress the right person at the right time with some titbit of knowledge, or feigned interest, but once it has served its purpose he will forget it. Likewise, he will dip his fingers in a varied and great number of business pies but withdraw his interest, and company cash, just as quickly for the next scheme, leaving business partners to go to the wall.

> I leave Hank at the front door, his arm round his fourth bride, Talita. Twenty years younger and a former Miss Italy, she is expecting her first and Hank's seventh child. Hank has already told me that he has set legal precedence with the tightest pre-nup in existence but, of course, 'I love her – just as much as any of my other brides. Isn't she great?' He pinches her bottom and she stifles an embarrassed yelp. At my last glance backwards, Hank gives me a big wink. Yes, he's the one who got the last laugh.

DO *YOU* HAVE WHAT IT TAKES TO BECOME A MULTI-MILLIONAIRE?

It would appear that in order to become a self-made million-aire, you need a number of characteristics that, outside the boardroom, would be recognised by a psychologist as some of the building blocks that make a psychopath. A ruthless will to succeed, an enormous ego, an almost delusional level of self-belief and a pocketful of dreams. Could you be one of those success stories too? Read the statements below and state whether you agree or disagree.

1. 'You won't become a self-made millionaire unless you believe that you will strike it rich one day. You should tell everyone you know that this is what is going to happen. When your bank manager demands the overdraft is repaid immediately, simply tell him not to worry – he's going to be managing a millionaire's bank account this time next year.'

2. 'I want people to believe that I have a phenomenal rags-to-riches story because it will polish my sheen of success – so it's OK to lie about my childhood. Instead of the suburban semi and two doctor parents, I talk about the lumps of coal we ate for Sunday lunch and the brown paper bags I wrapped round my feet for shoes.'

3. 'In my spare time I like to drive round Silverstone in an F1 car / swim with sharks while trailing a bloody steak behind me / play Russian Roulette with my shotgun.'

4. 'I've got lots of ideas that I know will make me rich – they haven't worked so far but I'm just going to keep trying until one does.'

5. 'I believe that the best way to get rich is to work for a man who is at the top of his game and take orders from him.'

6. 'I just clock in and clock out for work. I get the job done but I'm all about living for the weekend. I want to have fun and I'm saving for a wild and crazy summer holiday in Ibiza.'

7. 'Poverty is, in many cases, a form of mental illness.' (Charles-Albert Poissant in *How To Think Like A Millionaire*[10])

8. 'Life has tricked and thwarted me. I have denied my inner self for the sake of playing by the rules. In order to get rich I must break free.'

9. 'I refuse to recognise that there are impossibilities.' (Henry Ford)

10. 'You have to work hard to make money.'

Answers:

1. This statement indicates grandiosity – an essential psychopathic trait. But this is also a line frequently used in strike-it-rich seminars.

2. To agree here indicates a certain ruthlessness – is it OK to lie about your background to make your rise to riches even more impressive? Aristotle Onassis allowed everyone to believe he had an impoverished upbringing. In fact, his father was a prosperous merchant and president of the local bank.

3. This indicates a need for extreme stimulation – a tell-tale psychopathic trait. But equally, some of the self-made mega-rich, such as Sir Richard Branson, can frequently be spotted leaping out of an aeroplane or flying a hot-air balloon around the world.

4. Agreement here might indicate a psychopath who just doesn't seem to learn. But there again, it is often said that you can't keep a good man down. Several billionaires have seen their first few ventures fail; Donald Trump watched three of his business ventures go bankrupt but carried on regardless.

5. If you disagree, this would suggest a level of self-aggrandisement, a psychopathic tendency that the multi-millionaire Henry Ford shared. Having learned his trade at the Detroit Edison Company, he turned down a promotion and a raise in salary saying, 'I resigned, determined never again to take orders.'

6. Psychopaths are certainly work-shy but they would have no concept of saving for a holiday (although they are all for 'wild and crazy' nights out) – not when they can trick someone into taking them away for free.

7. Do you believe that being poor is just a state of mind? If you agreed with this statement, you probably have no

truck with people who blame their poverty on a paltry education or deprived background. Why can't they just find a way – *any* way – to get rich? As one of the molls in the Sky TV series *Gangster's Wives* said: 'If you want the nice things in life, you have to be a bit dodgy, don't you?'

8.   Agreement here certainly reveals a desire to get on and do what you really want to do (make a mint). But you are not psychopathic – a psychopath would never have conformed in the first place.

9.   Henry Ford brought the domestic car to millions in his own lifetime. He was told often that the mechanics and economics needed to make this happen were impossible; he overrode these beliefs. His level of self-belief, in which even the impossible was just another barrier to overcome, could be seen as psychopathic but it made him a millionaire. Agreeing here suggests that you might be rather deluded . . . but hey, then again you may really be onto something!

10.   Totally disagree? No, sorry, unless we win the lottery or inherit a fortune the majority of us have to work hard to earn our living. Psychopaths are typically drawn to get-rich-quick schemes. But if you want to be one of the super-rich bosses out there, you'd be better off heeding the maxim of Vince Lombardi, the famous American football coach: 'The dictionary is the only place that success comes before work.'

BERNIE MADOFF – THE $65 BILLION HEDGE-FUND FRAUDSTER

In June 2009, sixty-one-year-old Bernie Madoff was sentenced to 150 years in jail for fraud on a massive scale – the final estimate comes to nearly $65 billion (£40 million).

He had apparently run the most successful hedge fund in New York for several years, with high-profile investors such as Steven Spielberg, Kevin Bacon, HSBC and Santander (source: *Wall Street Journal*), but it unravelled when his clients started asking for their money back when the recession hit. The difficulty for Madoff was that there was no money to return: the entire company was one giant Ponzi scheme. Madoff had lived a life that included an Upper East Side apartment in New York, a $9.4 million home in Palm Beach, Florida, a 55ft yacht called *Bull* (a hint, perhaps, that all was not as it seemed?) and other luxuries on tap. Few appear to have suspected that this phenomenal hedge fund was, literally, too good to be true. But perhaps a closer look at this supposed financial genius would have unveiled psychopathic tendencies.

In *Madoff: The Man Who Stole $65 Billion*[11] author Erin Arvedlund relates a story about the young Bernie that demonstrates that his propensity for lying and cheating was not something that arrived with his twenty-first birthday. When a teenager at high school he was set the assignment of reading a book to talk about in class but he didn't bother to read anything. When called up, he spoke impressively about *Hunting and Fishing* by Peter Gunn – both names he made up on the spot. When asked to show the book, he coolly replied that he'd already returned it to the library. His classmates, on learning about the con, congratulated him.

Madoff was popular when living the high life but the judge sentencing him found it telling that he received no letters or pleas from friends testifying to his good deeds (he was renowned as a Jewish philanthropist before his arrest but big Jewish charities lost huge amounts in the fraud). There is a story that one widow, recently bereaved and ignorant about finance, went to Madoff to ask what she should do. He put his arm around her and said, 'Don't worry – your money is safe with me.'

ROBERT MAXWELL – THE MEDIA MOGUL WHO ROBBED HIS EMPLOYEES OF THEIR PENSION FUNDS

Robert Maxwell died in 1991 but the manner of his life and death has ensured his renown thirty years on. Born in the Czech Republic to a poor family, Maxwell moved to Britain in 1940 as a teenage refugee. In 1951 he made his first serious business purchase, buying a small publishing company. By 1980 he had acquired the British Printing Company (renamed as the Maxwell Communications Company) and in 1984 bought the Mirror Group Newspapers. By the time the nineties had arrived, Maxwell also owned Macmillan Publishing and 50 per cent of MTV Europe.

However, shortly after his body was found floating in the ocean – having apparently fallen off his yacht while cruising off the Canary Islands – the details of his financial dealings came to light. Hundreds of millions of pounds had been stolen from his own businesses – particularly from pension funds established for staff – to fund his over-ambitious corporate expansion plans and his lavish lifestyle. His son, Kevin, was later forced to declare bankruptcy with debts of £400 million.

It also transpired that in the weeks before his death he was being investigated by Scotland Yard's War Crimes Unit for allegedly killing German civilians in cold blood in 1945.

As early as 1973 – possibly even 1969, according to some sources[12] – after Maxwell's failed attempt to sell Pergamon Press (during which he lost control of it) the Department of Trade and Industry declared that he was 'not a person who can be relied upon to exercise proper stewardship of a publicly quoted company'. (Yet the following year he was able to borrow money to buy it back again.)

During his own lifetime, stories abounded of his huge charisma but also his quick temper and ability to keep staff in a more or less permanent state of fear. There is also a story, allegedly told by his children, which illustrates his lack of control: they came down one Christmas morning to find their father sitting amid a sea of discarded paper – he hadn't been able to resist unwrapping their presents.[13]

THE MYSTERY SURROUNDING CORPORATE BONUSES

In the 2007 PriceWaterhouseCooper survey ('Economic Crime: People, Culture and Controls'[14]) the company found that half of the 5,400 companies surveyed had been subject to some form of fiscal crime since the previous survey. Their average direct financial loss had risen 40 per cent, from $1.7million to $2.4million. They also found that the larger the firm, the more likely they were to fall victim to fraud: among those with 5,000 or more employees, 62 per cent suffered crime. Eighty-five per cent of the crimes were committed by men between the ages of thirty-one and fifty, and half of them had a college education or higher degrees. Half worked for the defrauded company, 26 per cent were in senior management and 43 per cent had worked for the company for more than five years.

In short, the PWC surveys support the suspicions of psychologists that psychopaths are likely to flourish in the world of senior corporate management. Larger firms appear to be more vulnerable to the predatory tactics of greedy criminals. Whether these corporations create a psychopathic atmosphere in their endorsement of high risk and competitive attitudes or whether that environment attracts psychopaths is another question.

SUMMARY AND ADVICE

It seems that many of the qualities that a successful entrepreneur is praised for are remarkably similar to many of the hallmarks of a psychopath: delusional self-belief, overbearing arrogance, single-minded ruthlessness in the pursuit of money, the ability to sell one's grandmother and a total insouciance when it comes to failure.

Should you suspect you are working for a true psychopath rather than someone destined to success and riches, we suggest the following ways of managing the situation:

- Ask yourself whether you are content to work in a high-risk environment for the rewards it offers you. If stability and job security are important to you, you may want to work for another company. Of course, there is always a certain amount of risk involved with any corporate job, as demonstrated during the recent recession where senior bankers took big risks that gave big pay-outs for years until the money ran out. There were a lot of greedy fat cats around but it doesn't make them psychopaths. Nor were most of the people working for them aware of the risks being taken with the company money. You need to make sure you are as informed as possible about the company you are working for before deciding whether or not the salary and pressure are worth it.

- Coping with a psychopathic boss on a more personal level (and sometimes simply changing departments may be enough to escape a manager from hell) requires you to proceed with caution. Understand what you are dealing with. While your customers or clients will be taken in by your boss's mesmerising pitch, you must remind yourself that it takes hard work, not just an over-active imagination, to be successful. As much as you can, you need to stay grounded about that because the hard work is likely to be yours.

- Never criticise your boss in front of anyone else if you want to keep your job. You can't reason with a psycho-pathic boss and they are very sensitive to anything that could be construed as an attempt to humiliate or under-mine them. Important issues should be discussed face to face and be careful to acknowledge everything they say and allow them to talk more about it before you put your view forwards. Always couch your opinion in terms of costs and benefits to your boss, as this is the only language they understand, and appeal to your boss's ego by allowing them to take credit for your insights.

- Maintain an amiable, professional relationship only with your boss. Resist being drawn into blurring boundaries between your private and work life. If, for example, you tell them about any of your own indiscretions during a drunken 'work drinks' be prepared to hear them repeated verbatim at the next office meeting.

- Finally, if you feel that you are working for a psycho-pathic boss then you cannot rely on the company for your future financial security. Be prepared to be sacked without notice, keep copies of any receipts for claiming expenses (in case they challenge you at a later date) and make independent pension arrangements. You should also keep any documents that may later protect you if anything should go to court – for example, emails from your boss containing unreasonable demands or relating to unprofessional conduct.

4

IS YOUR BEST FRIEND A PSYCHOPATH?

When you start a new job, move into a new area or you or your child start a new school you'll be keen to fit in. And that means making friends. Or perhaps you are already happily settled at work or in village life and someone new has arrived – and you'd like to help *them* fit in.

It's at just this moment of vulnerability that a psychopath can strike. Relying on your need to be liked – after all, who doesn't want to be popular? – the psychopath will become your 'friend', getting under your skin in order to infiltrate every area of your life. Before you know it, they've taken over your social life and your love life and probably drained your finances, leaving you isolated and exposed. They'll tell you that they are the only ones you can trust and the only ones who can help you out of the mess you're in. The very mess that they created.

It feels odd to me to tell this story because I'm not what you would call a victim. At least, I never thought I would be one. I live in one of the bigger houses in the village; I bought it after I sold my plumbing business for a decent profit a few years ago. (I've lived in the same area for over twenty-five years but I was lucky enough to be able to upsize my home.) I'm divorced but I see my teenage son, Charlie, regularly and I've got a pretty, slightly younger girlfriend, Elsie. When I go down to the local pub, there's always a chap or two to talk to – we all form a cricket team in the summer and enjoy a few matches on the village green.

And yet, despite all the trappings of my easy, semi-retired life, I got caught in a trap set by a con-man. For a long time, I truly thought Robert was my friend. Even now, I still can't quite believe that he's not. He seemed decent.

Robert moved to the village three years ago. He made an impact almost immediately. First of all, he was renting one of the biggest houses on the green. Secondly, he arrived in a beautiful vintage Bentley. Thirdly, he came to the pub on his first night and bought everyone in there a round. There were only about twenty or so customers but it was a nice gesture. I wasn't actually there at the time, but I found out later that he got chatting to Betty, the barmaid, and by cajoling her with some flattery he got all the village gossip out of her, finding out who was who and even who was doing what to whom. So I imagine that he had it in his head by the end of that night that I was the local big guy and he was going to make it his business to get to know me.

I first met him at our summer fete. He introduced himself and handed me a glass of Pimm's. I have to say, I was charmed at once. He's a good-looking fellow for his years and was well turned out in a pressed linen suit. Robert told me he was a property investor and had moved to our part of the world because it was 'untapped'. He was just renting because he wanted to get to know the area well before buying but we were soon under the impression that he had a couple of million to spend on the right place, just for himself. He said he wanted to get to know me because he had heard that I knew the place like the back of my hand and he thought that perhaps the two of us could do business.

Well, of course, I was intrigued and not a little flattered. I sent Elsie off to spend her pennies on the cake stall and he and I settled down for a drink in the pub garden. I soon discovered we had lots in common – at least, that's how it seemed. We'd both been brought up by our grandmothers (my mother had died, his had left his father when he was just a toddler); we shared the same middle name; we were a similar age and in our youth had followed the same bands and had

65

crushes on the same Playboy pin-ups. My hobby is collecting ships in bottles; his is nautical memorabilia. He told me that he had been an international yachtsman and even that he was a decorated lifeboat hero. We even discovered that we both have a deep love of Labradors. Of course, I have no idea now how many of these similarities are actually true.

Before long, Robert and I were meeting for a quick drink most nights, just to shoot the breeze. In some ways, it made me realise that perhaps I had been a bit lonely. I mean, I like the fellows from the village – I've known them for a long time – but it was fascinating to talk to Robert. He was so experienced and knowledgeable. I felt that here was a man who really understood me. We started talking business and I went on a few drives with him, spotting potential properties to buy and develop.

We looked around a few, and I thought he had a pretty good eye for an investment. Then, one day, he called me up to say that he'd been told by one of his trusted contacts, a property developer, that a really extraordinary deal was coming up in the Midlands. He was going to go and check it out. He then called me two days later to say that it was a goer – a buy-to-let property, and in an area that had lots of young couples looking to rent. We could buy it, rent it out for a year and then sell it on. We'd make a hefty profit on the rent alone. He said that as I'd been such a good friend to him so far, he'd like to split the deal with me. The only thing was that the contact wouldn't want anyone else coming in on it, so the best thing would be for me to write the cheque to him and then he would add his half and pay the developer directly. My share of the investment was to be £190,000.

I paid it. I didn't think I had anything to worry about at all and I was happy to invest my money well. Robert came back with brochures of the property and it did look very good. It looked bona fide. Only later did I discover that, of course, there was no property. The cheque was simply paid into Robert's bank account.

But it took me a year to realise. In the meantime, Robert and I did several more joint property investments together. None were as large as that first one but in total I invested close to £650,000 under Robert's guidance. It was money I had earmarked for my son's inheritance but I thought I was doubling the cash for him.

Still, even before I realised I'd been conned out of my money, I started to get little hints that all was not quite as it should be. It sounds silly, but I was talking to another chap in the pub and he was telling me what an aficionado of dachsunds Robert was, and that they had spent a jolly lunchtime pint discussing the finer points of the sausage-dog breed. I laughed and said, no, he isn't – Labradors are his dog. I brushed it off as a misunderstanding but it did prick at me a bit. Men don't get their dogs wrong.

Another evening, Robert brought a new lady friend to the pub. Chrissie was a wealthy divorcee and I was a little surprised that Robert was clearly chasing her. She was a perfectly nice woman but a bit brash and brassy. They were quite loud together in our quiet village pub and then he texted me a few days later to say that Chrissie had taken him off for a quick trip to Venice, where they were going to be staying at the Gritti Palace – the most expensive and classy hotel there. I definitely got the idea that she liked spending her ex-husband's money on Robert and that he was more than content to enjoy the lavish treatment. It didn't seem like my friend but I tried to be happy for him. Within a few weeks, Chrissie had moved into his house and we soon found out – village gossip, you know – that she was the one paying the rent.

Still, we kept meeting for our regular drink. Despite all the deals we were doing together, we didn't always talk business. Robert would largely entertain me with amusing tales of his past – the lifeboat rescues, the travelling around the world, the beautiful women he had romanced. He hinted that he'd been married more than a couple of times. He didn't talk about Chrissie much – in fact, if he did, it would make me feel a bit uncomfortable. He seemed a bit cold about her – making references to the bills she was paying for him and then laughing. But I just thought, 'each to his own', and brushed it off.

67

After we'd known each other for about a year, Robert told me that he and Chrissie were off to Barbados for a fortnight. I never saw him again. After about a month, I realised that not only could I not get hold of him (the phone was switched off, emails went unanswered), I had no idea how to trace the business deals we had done together: he had handled everything. Eventually, it was the estate agent who had rented him the house who got the police involved. Robert was wanted for fraud on a massive scale and I was just another of his victims. You'll think me a fool but I still don't know what upsets me the most – losing my money or losing my friend.

Geoffrey, 56, retired

Making a new friend can be as exciting as taking up with a new lover: you may find you want to spend all your free time with them, that hours are spent talking together as you excitedly discover more and more things that you have in common and you will even find yourselves making plans for the future. A true best friend comes along only rarely and may even last longer than your marriage. That special someone will be privy to all your secrets, will allow you to admit your failings without being judgmental and will support you in your hopes for the future.

A friendship with a psychopath is, of course, none of these things – they are incapable of empathy or loyalty to anyone but themselves. Yet they know what they need to do to make you believe that they are a better friend to you than anyone else. As we saw in the story above, Robert knew how to make Geoffrey feel that he had met a true friend: they had – on the surface at least – many things in common. Robert appealed to Geoffrey's vanity by identifying him as another 'top dog' in the village and, further, by asking him for help with local knowledge and finally, financial investment.

And so poor Geoffrey was more devastated by the betrayal of friendship than he was by the loss of his money, which is a completely normal response. Somehow, we all would rather believe that the friendship was real even if that person stole our cash. To admit to having 'fallen' for a new friend who turned out to be a fake would be to admit a gullibility and shame that is hard to bear. But you should not feel a fool: the psychopath is a wily character and he will have preyed on the softest parts of your soul.

The psychopath has the upper hand from the start because we are most likely to make new friends when we are anxious. We seek affiliation in conditions where we feel unsure of ourselves, whether it's because we have split from our partners, moved to a new area or started a new job. A classic study conducted in 1959 told female participants that they would be receiving electric shocks. Half were told that they would be painful, the other half that they would not. They were then given the choice of waiting either alone or with another person while the equipment was set up. The high anxiety group (i.e. the ones told it would be painful) were twice as likely to want company.[15]

Where you or I would usually choose a friend on the basis of having things in common, a psychopath chooses a 'friend' because that person has something that they want, or because that person can be useful to them. A psychopath does not always choose someone lowlier that they can pick on and manipulate – in fact, they often prefer the reflective glow of someone important, powerful or special in some way that will validate their own perceived social position.

When targeting someone, psychopaths have one clever trick up their sleeves. They are great mimics and will sometimes match someone's speaking patterns (their rate of speech, use of particular terms etc) and gestures. This in itself creates a rapport: we are unconsciously driven to feel more comfortable and to like someone who appears 'in sync' with us.

One rather endearing aspect of us non-psychopaths is that seeing someone we like doing something clumsy makes us like them more – perhaps because it makes them appear human. Psychopaths can give the impression of this, often inadvertently. They may slip up and make a social faux pas that belies their lack of connection with others but because they are not too fussed about it and may even laugh at the mistake, we like them for it. We tend to think, 'He doesn't take himself too seriously'. The very arrogant psychos are not so able to capitalise on this particular trick, however.

All relationships for a psychopath are about exploitation – they will use someone else in order to carry out their own desires. They do not, for example, understand the concept of doing a friend a favour, unless the favour is for them. Should you request a favour of them, they may either view it as 'money in the bank' (because they will ask a larger favour of you in return next week) or they will be insulted because they will see it as an invitation to be used, when they like to maintain the upper hand at all times.

Most dangerously, psychopaths use the confidential and personal information that friends exchange against the very person who confided in them. Those very tools of friendship – personal disclosure, intimacy, secrets – become weapons in the hands of the psychopathic best friend.

THE SEVEN SIGNS OF THE PSYCHOPATHIC BEST FRIEND

When Vanessa first met Heather she felt a little sorry for her. Heather was the new girl in an all-female PR firm: young, ambitious and a little overweight. Privately, Vanessa referred to Heather as 'Ugly Betty' – well-meaning, she thought, but badly dressed and in need of guidance. But despite the nickname she conferred on her friend, Vanessa was a kindly soul and she took Heather under her wing.

Within a few weeks, Vanessa and Heather were a tight clique of their own. They always went for lunch together and, encouraging Heather to lose her spare tyre, Vanessa always ordered the same sushi for them both. They went shopping together and Vanessa nudged Heather in the direction of the more trendy boutiques, egging her on to spend as much as her wages could stretch to. So it was almost inevitable when, just seven weeks after they met, Heather was forced to move out of her flat (her landlord was selling up, she said) and Vanessa offered her spare room – just until she found something else.

Now she was down a dress size, Heather took to borrowing Vanessa's clothes. Vanessa didn't really mind too much – until she noticed things were being put back dirty and smelling of cigarette smoke. But once she hadn't said something, it became harder to bring up the conversation. Then Heather showed no sign of looking for anywhere else to live, yet wasn't paying any rent to Vanessa – again, it just seemed too tricky a subject to bring up several weeks down the line. This would have been bearable but Heather thought nothing of using up all the hot water for her morning shower and would casually finish off Vanessa's Roquefort cheese or home-made marmalade, merely shrugging her shoulders if Vanessa said anything.

Sign I Imitation may be the sincerest form of flattery but Heather is behaving more like a parasite here. Heather has preyed on Vanessa cleverly, knowing that she will be too embarrassed to admit her goodwill has a limit. With no rent to pay, access to a wardrobe full of clothes and a fridge of delicious food – why would Heather move on? The final straw will be when Heather helps herself to Vanessa's boyfriend as easily as she dips her finger into her flatmate's taramasalata. At least, that would be the final straw if Vanessa ever found out about it.

Vanessa feels guilty for secretly resenting Heather and suppresses any nagging doubts – after all, friends share don't they? And Heather has now become her closest friend, or so she thinks. They work together, they live together and at the weekends they hang out together. They tell each other everything: the pair have shared every detail of their histories, from their first pet to their first love. At least Vanessa has. Heather has imparted bits of seemingly intimate information chosen to simply mirror her friend's life experiences, beliefs and feelings. In doing so, she has sent the message 'Look, we are just the same. . . you (and all your secrets) are safe with me'.

Sign 2 Heather is ingratiating herself as Vanessa's loyal and best friend – whilst all the time she is scheming to ensure that she never has to pay for anything again. She is giving Vanessa just enough of what she needs to hear in order to put all her trust in her. If Vanessa were to pay a little closer attention to the way in which Heather's stories are told, she might notice that they are rather lacking in subtlety and have something of the pantomime about them. They demonstrate all the hallmarks of psychopathic 'shallow affect'. Heather's tales of heartbreak are sketchy; her tears are noisy but wipe away quickly. She doesn't even have a photograph of the pet she expresses so much affection for.

As they get closer, Heather's confidence increases and Vanessa slowly realises that the tables are turning. She now relies on her friend for support. When Vanessa has a small falling-out with another girlfriend, Heather counsels her on how to respond. She suggests that Vanessa starts a rumour that the girl has genital warts. Vanessa laughs but is shocked and doesn't act on the advice. She has started to notice that Heather's treatment of others varies enormously. She had never thought of her friend as a bully but then again, she is just lovely to other friends, so she must just be looking out for her, right?

Sign 3 Because psychopaths view different people as having different worth to them, their behaviour towards them is disparate. This inconsistency is often hard to spot until they behave so disgustingly towards one individual that your attention is grabbed. At this point however, the 'out of character' treatment is readily justified or explained away. If the unfortunate victim is a common enemy, it is easier to collude with or ignore. You are secure in the belief that your soulmate would never turn on you after all.

WATCH THEIR HANDS

Psychopaths make more incidental hand gestures (known as 'beats') than non-psychopaths, particularly when discussing emotional or interpersonal matters, for example, descriptions of family relationships and early family life.[16] Psychologists believe that this might be a sign of the extra cognitive effort that they need to put into discussing feelings and concepts that are abstract to them. (Think of how you flap your hands about when searching for a word.) Criminal psychopaths show fewer beats when talking about the crimes they have committed, as these have been more fully experienced and hold more meaning for them.

Of course, access to Vanessa's flat, wardrobe and fridge is not enough for Heather. Pretty soon, she is muscling in on Vanessa's address book. She goes through Vanessa's friends, calling them to set up a 'surprise' lunch or drinks for their mutual friend, only to explain when she turns up without her that Vanessa was held up at work. Heather then switches on the charm and soon has the friends eating out of her own manicured hands. In the conversation Heather will slip in little 'confidences' – that 'poor Vanessa' is feeling under pressure at work; she is worried her boyfriend is having an affair; she is about to lose her top client account . . .

Slowly the friends start to take pity on Vanessa. Without really knowing how or why, she senses that she is losing her 'top dog' status as people start offering her help instead of looking to her for guidance. When someone at work lets slip that Heather has told them that she is worried about her friend, Vanessa confronts Heather. She is unfazed – I'm just looking out for you, she repeats. And adds for good measure that Vanessa needs someone looking out for her now. Vanessa bursts into tears. Of course, she says, you're my friend – please, help me.

Sign 4 Heather has expertly manipulated Vanessa – little by little in incremental stages so that Vanessa is hardly aware it is happening. Before she knows it, Vanessa has had her confidence severely undermined and, of course, the only person who can rescue her is her nemesis.

One day, Heather telephones Vanessa's parents. She explains to them that Vanessa is falling behind on her mortgage payments because she has failed to make the bonus she expected at work. Vanessa is too ashamed to call them herself, she says, and probably won't accept any help from them. But if they could give the money to Heather, she would be able to tell Vanessa that she is able to lend it to her (the parents, of course, assume that Heather is paying rent). The mother is a little sceptical and wonders if they shouldn't have Vanessa down for the weekend to talk it through. But the father is anxious that his daughter doesn't feel under pressure. He deposits enough to cover six mortgage payments in Heather's account. Of course, Vanessa never sees a penny.

Sign 5 Heather is quite happy to fleece both Vanessa and her parents without the slightest pang of remorse. Psychopaths are not sentimental about family ties, either their own or yours. To them, their so-called friend's and nearest and dearest are regarded as nothing more than additional resources to be drained.

One night, Heather suggests to Vanessa that they go to Ibiza for their summer holidays – a fortnight of clubs, beaches, men and sangria. What could be better? Vanessa agrees. The only problem is that she's used up all her holiday quota for the year (thanks to Heather's previous suggestions that they go to Prague for a mini-break, to stay in a country house hotel for another long weekend and then there was that time they flew to Dublin because they heard one of Heather's favourite film stars was staying there). Doesn't matter, says Heather, I've called work to say you've got gastric flu and used your credit card to buy the tickets – we're flying tonight . . .

Sign 6 What could be construed as a wild sense of zany fun and energy in some is the dangerous psychopathic tendency to impulsivity here. With no regard for the plans of others or even any proper sense of consequences, the psychopath just does what she wants, when she wants.

Heather and Vanessa jet to Ibiza but Vanessa's patience is beginning to wear thin with her friend. On holiday, Heather tries every drug and every cocktail she can – not to mention that she picks up a different bloke every night, leaving Vanessa either hiding in the bathroom with her hands over her ears or waiting in the hotel bar, biting her nails, until she gets the all-clear.

Then, on the last night, just as Vanessa is about to tell Heather that she can't stand a minute more of this outrageous behaviour, Heather drops a bombshell. She's got cancer, she says – that's why she's been living each day as if it was her last. Vanessa is, understandably, devastated. She sobs and pleads with her friend to let her look after her when they get home.

Only, this time, Heather hasn't been too clever. Waiting by the luggage carousel when they land back home, Heather leaves her handbag with Vanessa while she nips to the loo. Vanessa notices a letter from the local hospital peeking out and makes a spur-of-the-moment decision to read it – she wonders if Heather's cancer is even worse than she says. It would be just like her friend, she thinks, to underplay the whole thing so that Vanessa doesn't worry too much. But the letter reveals much worse than that. The lump that Heather went in to see them about is completely benign. There will be no further appointments required.

Sign 7 The breath-taking lie that Heather blurts out when confronted with the possible loss of her meal ticket is not your common-or-garden porky pie. Psychopaths lie with ease and will often 'over-pitch' a lie when they want to provoke a quick and helpful response from someone whose patience they may have already stretched. They are too callous to fully understand the emotional impact that such deception can have, and are content to toy with a friend's feelings as a cat will with a mouse if it yields the desired results. It is unlikely that Heather has initially given any thought to how she will perpetuate a tale of such magnitude but undoubtedly would have milked it as far as possible if she had been caught. Let's hope that for Vanessa's sake, this final error sends Heather out of her life. Of course, it will only send her straight into someone else's. Make sure it's not yours.

WATCH THEIR LIPS: HOW A PSYCHOPATH USES LANGUAGE

Psychopaths are typically described as possessing 'the gift of the gab' but it is the flair with which they speak that attracts our attention, rather than their eloquent use of words. In fact, experts have noticed peculiar and awkward features to the psychopath's use of language that might pass unnoticed by the more casual listener.

In his book *Without Conscience: The Disturbing World of the Psychopaths Among Us,* Hare describes 'frequent contradictory and logically inconsistent statements'. He quotes a convicted thief who, asked if he had ever committed a violent offence, replied 'No, but I once had to kill someone'. Psychopaths seem to put words together in strange ways – like malapropisms. Take for example the psychopath who describes himself as an 'escape goat' or 'victim of my own excess'.

Hare posits that it is 'as if psychopaths have difficulty monitoring their own speech', thereby allowing streams of convoluted and badly organised words and thoughts. When we speak it is the finale of a long sequence of complicated mental activity; so when a psychopath becomes garbled it is possible that his mental processes, just like his behaviour, are not bound by conventional rules.

It might be the case that the psychopath's idiosyncratic

style of speech is the product of an unusually 'lateralised' brain. In most people the left half of the brain has primary control over the way in which words are used and understood. But there is evidence to suggest that in psychopaths, the language centres are bilateral – i.e. located in both hemispheres.[18] This means that verbal information has to pass back and forth between the two halves of the brain and may therefore become more easily muddled.

THE LAWS OF FRIENDSHIP AND HOW A PSYCHOPATH EXPLOITS THEM

In an article on the psychology of friendship Karen Karbo outlines some basic laws of friendship from a mix of classic studies and recent research.[19] A clever con-man could use these laws to create a false friendship: understand them yourself and you could be more effectively protected.

1. The law of regularity: you tend to become friends with someone you see regularly. One study followed friendships in a single two-storey apartment building. Unsurprisingly perhaps, people were most likely to be friends with close neighbours and least likely with those on a different floor. A psychopath will ensure that he crosses your path frequently, building a repertoire of familiarity that leads as if naturally to friendship.

2. The law of reciprocity: in any relationship we rely on the law of reciprocity – where we give a little in exchange for something in return. The nicer among us are embar-

rassed not to return something given to us by a friend –
potential or otherwise – whether it's information,
compliments, emotional support, help or even money.

3.   The law of intimacy: in establishing a friendship we
     confer secret desires, talk freely of our history and
     divulge our hopes for the future. It is often the extent
     to which we freely extend our most intimate thoughts
     that determines the parameters of the friendship. A
     psychopath will apparently tell you his innermost secrets
     (they will, naturally, be completely made up) in order to
     encourage you to do the same (according to the law of
     reciprocity), thus drawing you in ever deeper into his
     circle.

4.   The Ben Franklin Effect: this is the name of the law
     devised by former American president Benjamin Franklin,
     noted that, 'He that has once done you a kindness will
     be more ready to do you another than he whom you
     yourself have obliged.' In other words, if you do something
     nice for someone you tend to believe that you must
     have done so because they are worth doing
     something for . . . and therefore you will again. You even
     feel more obligated towards someone you have helped
     than towards someone who has helped you. So the
     psychopath who encourages you to do him a favour, can
     depend on you performing another . . . and another . . .
     and another . . . and yet has no need to do any for you.

5.   The law of social-identity support: this law describes how
     we often choose our friends because they support our
     own social view of ourselves. So, while we may believe
     that so-and-so is a friend because of who they are, in
     truth it is because they bolster our identity. Mothers will
     be friends with other mothers; churchgoers will stick

together; celebrities would rather hang out with each other, and so on. This also works at the more dodgy end of the scale – drug addicts would rather stay friends with those who condone their vices than with those who are urging them to break the habit, even though the latter set of friends is clearly demonstrating greater love than the former. A psychopath will deliberately establish himself as a supporter of your social identity – you will probably meet him at the school gates, in your gym or at the tennis club. It will also help the psychopath that it is in precisely those places where you feel relaxed – because you fit in there – that your guard will be down, allowing him to move in with ease.

PETER FOSTER – THE MAN WHO GOT CHERIE BLAIR INTO TROUBLE

Even people in the most powerful and protected positions are not immune from the wiles of a con-man, as Cherie Blair, wife of then UK Prime Minister Tony Blair, found to her considerable cost in 2002.

In 2007 Peter Foster was sentenced to four and a half years in an Australian jail for fraud; he had admitted to obtaining £130,000 from a Micronesian bank, claiming it was for a property development but then using it to pay off credit card debts. Previously, Foster has been jailed in three other continents for selling bogus slimming products and using false documents.

In his past he claims to have been earning more money than his teachers by the age of fifteen, when he ran a business leasing pinball machines to apartment blocks in Queensland. At seventeen, he was the 'world's youngest boxing promoter' when he staged a world elimination title fight featuring the then British and European light-heavyweight champions. At twenty he was fined for attempting a fraudulent insurance claim; the following year he was declared bankrupt. Later, he became a television producer and filmed a documentary with Mohammed Ali while living with Ali at his home near Wilshire Boulevard in LA. He then started selling a diet tea, Bai Lin, and in marketing this product got Sarah, Duchess of York and glamour model Samantha Fox to endorse it and became a major sponsor of Chelsea FC. Samantha Fox said of Foster: 'Sure, he later turned out to be a scumbag, but when I met him he was this smooth, good-looking entrepreneur who taught me about life.' In 1996, he was jailed for breaching laws over distribution of the tea, only to abscond nine months later to Australia (he was subsequently re-arrested and extradited back to the UK).

He had also been an undercover operative for the Australian Federal Police in the 1990s and claimed to have been one for the British police force, too. Despite this chequered past, Foster managed to appoint himself 'financial advisor' to Cherie Blair, when he became her friend through his girlfriend, the Downing Street's unofficial fitness guru, Carole Caplin. In 2002, having officially denied – more than once – that the dodgy Foster had had anything to do with her private financial affairs, Cherie Blair was forced to admit just days later that he had in fact advised her on the purchase of two flats in Bristol. The issue was that it was not considered right that the wife of the Prime Minister should have taken the advice of a convicted con-man to negotiate a cut-price deal on her properties.

Blair did her best to distance herself from Foster but an email was revealed in the *Daily Mail* in which she described him as 'a star' and said: 'We are on the same wavelength, Peter.' Caplin later said of her ex: 'He is just a fantasist and these absurd stories shouldn't be given any credibility.'

Most recently, in 2009, Foster has claimed to want to broker a peace deal between Australia and Fiji.

Many people will measure their success in their life according to the friendships they have made and many would concur that a few close friends are better than a thousand acquaintances. It is for these reasons that when someone comes along who appears to have all the right qualities to be our friend we will invest heavily in the relationship. Which is why a 'friendship' with a psychopath can be so damaging when we discover it was built on a foundation of lies. It is this betrayal of trust that can feel more hurtful than even the pain of money stolen.

What is interesting is how psychopaths learn to exploit the friendly nature of their victims despite the fact that the very terms and conditions of friendship imply lots of things of which a psychopath has no concept: trust, warmth, loyalty, support and so on. It may be that it is not so much the language of friendship that a psychopath learns to deadly effect but that he instead has an understanding of how to exploit some apparently fundamental laws of friendship.

It can be difficult to tell if a psychopath has targeted you for your friendship – after all, self-disclosure is a risk we all have to take in the first stages of any relationship. But there are questions you should ask yourself: are they asking you for bigger and bigger favours without doing anything for you in return? Are they putting you down in public? Do they encourage you to end your friendships with other people or are they using your contacts to benefit their own address book? True friendship is about both giving and receiving: does yours have the right balance?

Psychologist Debra Oswald PhD at Marquette University in Milwaukee, USA, says there are four behaviours which are necessary to maintain the bonds of friendship: self-disclosure and ongoing supportiveness (both of which are necessary for intimacy), interaction (you need to phone, email or visit your friends) and being positive (a rewarding friendship motivates us to keep it alive). In order to kill a damaging friendship you need to stop doing these four things. A psychopath will find it hard to lure you in if you refuse to give them intimate information, if you do not call them and if you are not supportive of their plans or desires.

Luckily, friendships with psychopaths tend to be short-lived for obvious reasons. Heather would be unlikely to cry when her friend Vanessa wises up and dumps her – she, after all, doesn't have a need for the company and approval of others, just the benefits they can bring her.

5

IS YOUR DATE A PSYCHOPATH?

In matters of the heart we need to be especially cautious. It's in those moments of attraction that our defences are down and that's when the psychopath can strike. The dates they take you on may be exciting for being different but an element of fear could increase your attraction to them. The fixed intense stare of a psychopath may be more alluring than you realise. Even keeping a date casual and light with a psychopath can be hard: they are prone to expressing deep emotions fast – and if you want somebody to love, that could be the hook that reels you in.

If you've been on a few dates, you're almost certain to have had one bad one. But how do you know whether it's just a date gone wrong or an encounter with a psychopath?

During dinner, my date seemed to prefer talking to the waitress than to me. The final straw was when he took her phone number as he paid for the bill.

On the first date, he told me I'd look great pregnant.

I met one date at an 'elite singles' event, only for him to tell me later that he was married. And he didn't even understand why that was inappropriate.

When he showed up, he was five years older and five stone heavier than his Internet picture, sat smoking into my face and took a phone call from his mate during the evening so I could hear him declare that I was 'well fit'. And when asked if he reckoned he was going to get me into bed, said: 'Yeah, I reckon so, mate.' He also bragged about his beloved Jag all night long, only to reveal I wouldn't be getting a lift home in it at the end of the date: he'd been done for drink driving.

I went on a date with a property developer who, half an hour in, said: 'I can't wait for you to see my house. You can decorate it any way you want!'

We were at a pub for our first date, when he saw a group of his friends arrive. 'Don't look round,' he said to me, 'but I don't want my friends to see me with you. I'll go and talk to them while you slip out. I'll come and meet you round the corner in 20 minutes.'

After the date – just one date – she emailed me to say she'd printed out a photo of me and had put it in a frame to put on her desk at work.

I couldn't understand why my date was ushering me out of the restaurant so quickly. I soon realised when he grabbed my hand and started running. He hadn't paid.

Various daters, all ages

With the steep growth of online dating in recent years, the need to be vigilant about exactly who you're planning to share a bottle of wine with is greater than ever. A psychopath can hide his true self behind a computer screen with ease. Prolific liars, they will think nothing of telling you what you want to hear in order to seduce you into giving them what they want. And you can't necessarily rely on your normal filters, such as checking their shoes. Psychopaths, after all, come in all guises: from the giro-cheque scrounger to the millionaire in a Versace suit.

Added to the challenge is the fact that a cunning psychopath will fool you: he'll be charming, immensely flattering and often tell you well-practised compliments. Even the American serial killer, Ted Bundy, who confessed to over thirty murders committed between 1974 and 1978, had a girlfriend or two. You might go on a date with a psychopath and at the start of the night you could be thinking: 'What a lovely fella!' He'll most likely show up with a big bunch of flowers, showering you with compliments. It's only halfway through the date – perhaps just as you're wondering whether or not to have that chocolate mousse – that you'll start to ask why some things just aren't adding up. And if you do query his stories, it's not so much the lies he tells as the response that matters. A non-psychopath, caught out in a white lie, will blush like a goosed matron. But a pathological liar will simply wave away your puzzlement as if a fly in the ointment.

The key factor in a psychopath's make-up is his inability to feel empathy. So, in a situation where he should be trying his hardest to make you feel comfortable and that you have lots in common, he will fail. If your date fails to register any sympathy when you tell him that your cat died last week – take note. If your date is smarmy and fails to notice that this is making you ill at ease – that's another red flag. And if your date tells you that he is into slasher movies, extreme porn or animal torture, yet doesn't register the look of horror on your face . . . Well, you know not to give him your phone number, don't you?

You are not helpless. The most important thing to remember is that when you encounter a psychopath on a charm offensive the best defence is your own sense of self-esteem. A psychopath might choose someone with a higher status or better job than them (they like the kudos) but they will only succeed in victimising someone who is vulnerable. Know your boundaries and if your date crosses them in a way that makes you uncomfortable, walk away.

Every single friend I have – male or female – who has tried Internet dating has a tale to tell. Perhaps some of the dating stories in this chapter just seem funny, and in some ways they are, but it's not so funny if you end up actually getting involved with a psychopath. I am seeing a rise in the number of my clients who meet people on chat sites or over the Internet, just as you would expect as the Internet grows in usage and popularity. The three key things that make the Internet so attractive to my criminal clients are:

1. The *anonymity* it allows: I had one client who managed twenty separate email accounts to take on twenty different online personas, which ranged from a twelve-year-old girl to a seventy-year-old grandfather.

2. The *instant gratification* it gives them: you can make contact with someone at the touch of a button, rather than having to go out and try to meet them in a bar or at work.

3. The *accessibility* it gives them: the Internet puts the psychopath in front of a huge volume and variety of people it would otherwise take him several lifetimes to meet.

With this in mind, let's take a look at how you might see the signs of a psychopath while Internet dating.

THE SEVEN SIGNS OF THE PSYCHOPATHIC DATE

Susie has just turned forty and is recovering from her divorce, which went through a year ago. She doesn't have any children but it was a pretty bruising experience. Her friends are encouraging her to get back into the dating scene. Susie is nervous but thinks that she probably should give it a go. She'd like to find love again, with a nice, kind man who makes her laugh and adores her for who she is. Despite her divorce, she basically thinks men are OK and is willing to trust in the hope of a new relationship. She logs on.

The first chap to send her an online 'wink' is Roger007. She likes the look of his picture (dark hair, blue eyes, cheeky grin) and 'winks' back. Within an hour he has sent her an email and she is impressed by his witty charm. Just a few emails later and Roger007 is confessing that he has fallen for her – hook, line and sinker. 'You're the one I'm dreaming of,' he writes. 'I can't live without your love.'

Susie feels a bit overwhelmed by this. She wants someone to be mad about her but, if anything, he's being a bit too keen. Still, she thinks, she deserves someone nice. So she emails back encouragingly, if not in quite the same tone.

The emails keep coming. For the most part, they are nice, with Roger writing about his day and walks with his dog. But in the last paragraphs there are some rather overly heartfelt lines. 'You're all these arms of mine wanna hold,' he says. 'Baby, I'm giving you this heart of gold.'

Something about this is not quite right. But Susie can't put her finger on it. She thinks perhaps he is just very in touch with his emotions. Then she gets what turns out to be the final email from Roger007. It is brief. 'Every night in my dreams, I see you, I feel you,' he says. 'That is how I know you go on.'

Roger007 isn't crazy in love – he's just using Celine Dion song lyrics. Susie sensibly blocks him from her account.

Signs 1 and 2 Roger007 has displayed the psychopathic trait of superficial charm. A psychopath has no natural feelings of loving empathy. In order to say what they know a lover wants to hear, they will simply mimic words they find elsewhere. As they are also keen to manipulate a potential sexual partner into doing what they want, they will profess love or high emotion early on. What they're saying is not what they're feeling, so they may get the pitch wrong. This display of shallow emotion is known as 'shallow affect' and is what makes them appear 'too keen'. If you feel they're falling in love too quickly – you're wrong. They're not falling in love at all.

Still, Susie isn't put off. There's always one, she thinks. Next up is Harry69. The clue, she realises later, is in the name. He starts off pleasant enough – he loves long walks in the countryside and is looking for a long-term relationship – but by the third email he mentions other women from the site that he is chatting to and makes her feel as if he is only interested in sex, and fast. On the fourth email he is suggesting a threesome and bragging of the time he slept with two gorgeous twin sisters. Also, does she like the website hotsex999.com? Another block. Bye-bye, Harry69.

Sign 3 Psychopaths are prone to boredom, desiring stimulation – promiscuous sexual behaviour is one way to deliver this. They won't understand that suggesting pornographic sex before you've even gone on a date is inappropriate. As far as they see it, they are simply looking to fulfil their needs and you might be able to help them.

Poor Susie. She's not having too much luck. Perhaps a man might do better? Ronnie is a young man in his twenties and works too hard to meet anyone. When he goes to bars, he finds it difficult to make a judgement about someone over just one or two drinks: he'd rather get to know someone slowly over a few emails. Dairylea1976 seems sweet. She has a slightly hopeless expression in her photograph, which Ronnie finds endearing. She needs looking after, he thinks.

Quickly, they find that they are opening up to each other. Dairylea1976 tells him that she had a troubled childhood and was in and out of detention centres from the age of thirteen. But this was only because she was trying to escape a father who beat her and a brother who used her as a scapegoat for his own misdemeanours. A short spell in prison when she was twenty was unfortunate, she says – a friend planted some cocaine on her and the police raided the pub they were in. But she's learned her lesson and now she's trying to turn her life around.

Sign 4 Ronnie feels sorry for Dairylea1976. But he should be on the alert. Early behavioural problems are a red flag, a warning sign he shouldn't ignore, not to mention that she blames all her criminal convictions on others.

Ronnie reassures her that he understands what she's been through – he had some tough times in his childhood too. Besides, haven't we all had a run-in with the police at one time or another? He tells her that she is doing well to get back on her feet after all that. Still, he does feel that he'd like to get to know her a bit better before meeting. So when she suggests that they meet for a date, he is hesitant. Perhaps in a few weeks, he says, when they've emailed and talked a bit more.

But Dairylea1976 is upset by this. Please, she says, come on a date with me soon. And then she reveals something truly shocking: she has just six months to live. She didn't want to tell him but she really likes him and she's afraid that if they don't meet soon, she'll miss out on this last chance of love.

Sign 5 This, of course, is not true. Dairylea1976 is conning Ronnie into a date. The 'six months to live' line might sound extreme, but it happened to a client of mine – out of sympathy, he went on the date. Any play on emotion on a first date is a sign of manipulation: a ploy by the psychopath to get you to do what she wants. Watch out for sob stories too early on (wouldn't you normally save them for later, after you've put your best foot forward?), likewise extreme flattery or any kind of behaviour that is designed to make you feel as if you owe them something. If, for example, they make a huge fuss about paying for the dinner or having travelled for miles to meet you, they are being manipulative. It's a first date, for goodness' sake! They should be excited, not acting as if they're doing you a big favour.

What of a more typical tale, perhaps – two online daters who meet only to find that one of them looks absolutely nothing like his photo. Our Internet candidate, Penguin89 is at least a stone heavier and a foot shorter than his profile picture portrayed. He is not in the least apologetic about this – he uses his brother's photo, he explains, because otherwise he'd never get any responses on the site. His date, Jennifer, would be disappointed by this but she'll probably acknowledge that he is hardly the first person to cheat with his online image. But it's the other funny things that ought to put her a little on edge. Stories that Penguin89 had told her on email – like the job his father had, where he went to prison and what for, the job he has now, even his nephew's name and where he went for his last summer holiday – are contradicted in conversation. When Jennifer points out that he said he went to the Galapagos Islands last summer, not the Costa del Sol, Penguin89 just laughs and says, 'Oh yes, you're right. No, I didn't go there.' Disarmed by this response, she lets it go.

Sign 6 Penguin89 is a pathological liar. It's one thing to post a picture of yourself ten years ago, quite another to use someone else's image. And his ease with brushing off stories that don't quite tally is the classic response of a practised liar. Jennifer decides to give up on the date, swiftly downs the rest of her G&T and makes her way home, where she will log on and block Penguin89 from any further contact.

Then we take a man like Brian, who has had something of a midlife crisis recently and is also having a hard time finding the right girl online. But he is hopeful about the newest addition to his inbox. He's hoping his luck will change with Lobster4. After all the emotional intensity of previous cyber dates, Lobster4 is an intriguing change. She's quite a bit younger but says she likes an older man and Brian decides he could do with a bit of light-hearted fun. There's no talk of a job but she has an impressive list of hobbies: extreme skiing, white-water rafting, rock climbing, motorbike rallies . . . Surely, she must have money to be able to indulge in those activities? After just a few emails, Lobster4 suggests that he comes to pick her up the next morning for a day out. Perhaps even a few days away? She knows a lovely hotel in Brighton. They could have a picnic on the beach and go clubbing in the evening. Brian is alarmed. It's March and it's cold. He hasn't been to a nightclub for years and as for spending a few days with someone he hasn't so much as shared a bottle of wine with . . .

Brian has had enough. He deletes his account with the website, calls a friend and goes to the local pub instead. He's always rather fancied his friend's sister. Perhaps now is the time to discuss it with him over a pint or two.

Sign 7 Brian was right to follow his instincts about Lobster4. While someone successful and go-getting may well share her list of hobbies, what he would have been bound to discover soon was that she had only tried each of those things once or twice before getting bored. This – plus her desire to be taken away so soon and indulge in pastimes that were inappropriate – are signs of an extreme need for stimulation. Lobster4 was never going to hang around for Brian.

ARE YOU DATING A PSYCHOPATH?

Here are the profiles of four first dates – can you spot the psycho?

Type A: You met him online – he's already told you that you're the most gorgeous girl he's ever seen. For your first date you didn't particularly fix anything up – you met him by the station and just went to the first pub you saw. The first thing he said when you met was how stunning you looked and if he could touch your hair. At the pub he orders two pints and two tequila chasers. You start to chat and get to know each other. He says he likes off-piste skiing and drag-car racing. As more wine is drunk, he reveals that he generally feels put-upon in life and that his family hate him. The conversation moves onto politics – you realise that you have opposing views on the current government. But as soon as you say this, he backtracks and says, no, he sees your point and, when he thinks about it, he agrees with you after all. Just before the main course is over, the wait-ress comes over to top up the wine and accidentally spills some onto your date's trousers. He asks her what the hell she thinks she's doing and demands to speak to the manager – he wants the meal taken off the bill. The manager says he can't discount the whole meal but he will take the wine off the total amount. But when you're putting your coat on, leaving your date to – you assume – pay the bill, he grabs your hand and starts running. Outside, a little breathless, your date suggests that you both go back to his place. It's OK, he says, he's got condoms.

Type B: You met him through a friend who knows you both and thought you'd be perfect for each other. For your first date he booked a table at a local restaurant and picked you up at 7.30 p.m. He told you that you looked 'lovely' and opened the car door for you. At the bar before dinner, he buys the drinks but sticks to non-alcoholic beverages for himself because he's driving. You discover that his hobbies are fishing and chess, that his mum and dad are happily retired and that he'd like to go on holiday to Spain this year. When you start to discuss politics and discover that you think differently he says that you have a fair point but he is sticking to his guns. When the waitress spills wine on his trousers, he waves her apologies away and dabs at his trousers with a napkin. The meal over, the bill arrives and he waves away your attempts to pay, saying, 'This one's on me – you can get the next one, perhaps?' At the end of the night he offers to drop you home, gives you a kiss on the cheek and asks if he can call you again.

Type C: You met him in a bar – he complimented you on your beautiful hair and asked if he could buy you a drink. For your first date he collected you in a sports car and suggested a drive to the seaside even though it was mid-winter. He said that you looked stunning and asked what colour underwear you had on. You stop off at a pub on the way to the coast but leave quickly when it looks as if he's about to pick a fight with the barman; he thought you were flirting with him. In his free time he likes to try out any kind of extreme sports and watches horror movies. He even brags that he gets into fights now and then, but he always wins. When you mention politics and offer a view on the Prime Minister's latest foreign policy statements, he gets angry quickly and says that you clearly don't know what you're talking about. When the wine is spilled on him, your date tells the waitress to f*** off as she dabs at his trousers. Then he grabs your hand and says you're both leaving – the bill won't be paid. You go back to his place for more wine and have sex with him on the sofa. Immediately after he's finished he asks you to leave. As you're going through the door he says he'd like to see you again tomorrow night but it will be late – he'll come by after his boys' night out.

Type D: You met after he answered your ad in the 'personals' section of the local newspaper. You arranged the first date – a meal at a Michelin-starred restaurant that you'd always wanted to go to. He looked a bit crestfallen that you had booked some-where but said perhaps for the next date you could go to the place he had thought of. When you chat he says he doesn't really have any hobbies but when you mention that you like rock climbing he says he'd like to get into that. Otherwise, he's pretty quiet, saying he'd rather not talk about himself but hear about you. Testing the water with a little light political discussion, he offers his view but when he realises that you think completely differently he apologises and says you're probably right and he's wrong. When you see the waitress spill the wine on his trousers you immediately ask to see the manager and demand that the dry-cleaning bill is paid. Your date says nothing. At the end of the meal, the bill arrives and you pointedly leave your date to pick it up. He blanches at the total but he pays up. At the end of the night, he drives you home and you suggest that he comes up for coffee.

Answers:

A. If your date fitted the signs in type A, you are not dating a psychopath but there are definite signs of behaviour that would be aggressive and damaging to those around him. It would be best to decline a second date.

B. If your date sounds just like type B then you are probably dating your average nice guy. But it's also possible to see here that while he is a decent person he might sometimes not appear to be as exciting as the bad psychopath. You need to weigh up whether in the long run a steady, kind person is better to be with than the exciting but nasty one.

C. If you recognise the behaviour in type C as being all too familiar then you should steer clear. This is a classic psychopath who likes risk-taking with no regard for his or your safety, is parasitic, has poor behavioural controls, an over-developed sense of entitlement and is likely to indulge in criminal activity. Don't set up another date. Ignore his phone calls.

D. If your dates sound mostly like the one with type D then you're definitely not going out with psychopaths. If anything, you are possibly exerting rather too much of your own will over the dates you choose. Perhaps you had better take a long, hard look at yourself before you choose your next romantic partner.

DAVID CHECKLEY – THE INTERNET FRAUDSTER

David Checkley from Mill Hill in London was jailed in September 2010 for swindling more than thirty women out of a total of £500,000 in an Internet dating scam. Many of these women lost substantial sums and one even lost her home. Checkley, fifty-three, arranged blind dates over the Internet and then set about cheating the women with a number of sob stories. He told some he was a terminally ill Parkinson's sufferer and others that he had been a fighter pilot in Vietnam. He would then ask them for money. In some cases it was for medical treatment. In others, he claimed to be a successful architect or property developer who needed money for a project. In some instances, when the women smelled a rat and asked for their money back, he would threaten them in an effort to silence them. The women were bowled over by his charm, convinced by his stories and ultimately intimidated by his threats.

The good news for psychopaths is that when people are aroused by fear or anxiety any feelings of attraction are increased. This was the conclusion of a startling piece of research carried out in 1974 by Arthur Aron, a psychologist at Stony Brook University, New York. On the Capilano Canyon Suspension Bridge in Vancouver, British Columbia – a narrow, rickety bridge of wooden slats and wire cable suspended 230 feet above rocks and shallow rapids – unsuspecting men aged between eighteen and thirty-five years old crossed over. About halfway across, they would bump into a good-looking woman, brandishing a questionnaire, who told them that she was researching beautiful places. She would ask a few questions and give the man her phone number in case he wanted to know the results.

The same experiment was then carried out – using the same attractive researcher – on another bridge that was wide and steady and only ten feet above a rivulet.

The result: men crossing the suspension bridge rated the woman more attractive and about half of them called her. Only two of the sixteen men on the sturdy bridge gave her a call.

In short – fear got the men's attention and aroused emotional centres in their brains. It's certainly an original pick-up tactic. The theory is that people misinterpret fearful or anxious bodily arousal for sexual arousal in some circumstances. Hence, if you take a date to a scary movie, they are more likely to fancy you.

But whereas a non-psychopath might put you through a mild level of over-arousal that is entertaining (say, a ride on the big dipper), in the hope of some first-date action,[20] a psychopath will drive at 100 m.p.h. to the restaurant for their entertainment, not yours. In other words, if they start laughing at your fear, they're not doing it for your benefit.

I met Harry when he approached me at a smart country club. Despite the fact I was surrounded by friends, he was unfazed and asked me for my number. Not wanting to embarrass him in front of everyone, I gave it to him. When he called the next day, I said I was sorry but I couldn't meet him after all. He called twice more, and I said the same thing again. Harry kept calling. After five more calls, I agreed to meet him in a fortnight's time and planned simply to cancel. 'Surely then he would get the message,' I thought. But I forgot about the date as I was busy at work and suddenly the moment had arrived. In haste and furious with myself, I arrived at the club and Harry escorted me to the canteen. While he was getting lasagne and red wine, I bumped into an old school friend. When the friend realised that I was there with Harry, her mood changed. 'Get out of here now!' she hissed. I was bemused. 'He's put two women in hospital,' my friend said. 'He's a danger. If you resist his advances, he gets angry. Walk away.' By this time, Harry was bearing down on us with the tray of food. I ate my supper in four minutes flat and then said I'd be going. Harry looked surprised. 'I've got a boyfriend,' I lied. 'I shouldn't be here.' Darkness was beginning to fall, so I walked quickly to my car as Harry ran behind. With my hand out in front, I told him to back off. 'Do not follow me to my car,' I instructed. 'So — when can we do this again?' he called.

INTERNET DATING – THE PSYCHOPATH'S PLAY-GROUND?

In recent years, there has been a huge, unprecedented growth in online dating. Where once it was seen as a last resort for the desperate, now it is as routine and acceptable as going down to your local bar. For every kind of person you might want to date, there's a website to find your cyber-mate. Whether you live in a large, anonymous city or a rural hinterland, these websites are manna from heaven.

But – just as in real life – there are people online who are good and others who are bad. As you would protect yourself in the real world, you need to protect yourself in the virtual one. Don't give too much of yourself away too soon. Try to take a light-hearted approach to any flirtation. Don't judge too quickly whether someone is 'The One'. The last thing you need to do is approach every potential online date as the one who is going to fill an aching void in your life. It's that vulnerability that will mark you out as easy prey.

It's much easier online for people to create identities for themselves that they can hide behind. That beautifully crafted witty email? It probably *was* carefully honed – and in person they will only fail to replicate that repartee and turn of phrase – then copied and pasted and sent to several different cyber profiles. Treat any photograph with caution (even the most honest of us is going to send in the most flattering picture we can). Check for consistency in background stories. Most importantly of all – wait until you meet offline to verify what you really feel.

FIRST DATE WARNING SIGNS

A quick checklist: if your date ticks off half or more of these signs, which are aligned to traits in the PCL-R (see Chapter One), you're in the danger zone.

- A white mark where the wedding ring should be = *Pathological liar*

- Drives his own car too fast or drunk, even when you ask him not to = *Irresponsibility*

- Chatted you up in the street = *Impulsivity*

- Expects you to bask in his glory = *Grandiosity*

- Changes opinion too quickly so he can agree with you = *Shallow affect*

- or . . . is overly aggressive when you disagree with them = *Poor behavioural control*

- Is nice to you but rude to the waitress or cab driver = *Superficial charm*

- Borrows money to pay for the date = *Parasitic*

- Assumes there's going to be sex at the end of the date = *Sense of entitlement*

- Talks about moving in with you during the first date = *Parasitic or Impulsive*

- Doesn't see that you are uncomfortable with their high level of emotional intensity or smarminess = *Lack of empathy*

- Tells stories in which they are the tragic victim or valiant hero of the story = *Narcissistic*

- Doesn't ask you any questions about yourself = *Overly high sense of self-worth*

IS IT LOVE OR HORMONES?

A study of mental health professionals who have cause to interview psychopaths as part of their job found that they reported a range of fear and anxiety-related physical responses to them, including a sick feeling in their stomach, muscular shakes, palpitations and goosebumps.[21] All of which sounds rather similar to the feelings one might experience on a first date.

But perhaps hormones explain the responses. Anecdotal evidence suggests that many psychopaths tend to maintain a fixed, intense stare, which makes it difficult to decipher their feelings. People can feel confused and intimidated by it, which helps the psychopath to control and dominate them.

But how can you tell if your date is a psychopath, eyeing you up as dinner, or if he just really fancies you (and is eyeing you up in anticipation of dessert)?

When we are attracted to someone, we tend to gaze into their eyes. This triggers the release of oxytocin, the 'love hormone', which stimulates feelings of romantic bonding and sexual desire. Even in the absence of an initial attraction, 'the look' can be powerful stuff. Professor Arthur Aron, of the State University of New York at Stonybrook, put strangers of the opposite sex together for 90 minutes and had them discuss intimate details about themselves. He then asked them to stare into each other's eyes for four minutes without talking. Many of the subjects reported a deep attraction for their partner after the experiment, and two of them even ended up getting married six months later.

Oxytocin levels tend to be rather higher in women, particularly when in their twenties. So, ladies, if a psychopath is fixing you with a stare, don't stare back – or the following morning you could be wondering how you ended up in bed or married to them.

THE 'HALO EFFECT'

The 'halo effect' is a term used by social psychologists to describe the attribution of all kinds of qualities to a person based on their looks. It is so called because we allow one or two traits to overshadow all others, just as a halo does as an optical light effect or in religious images. Generally, we imagine good-looking people to have better personalities, to be warm in character and even good in bed. The effect is most likely to occur when we don't have enough information about a person – for example on a first date or with only a dating profile to go on.

We also tend to forgive or excuse the behaviour of a good-looking person more readily: studies have found that attractive court defendants are less likely to be found guilty.[22] There are various theories as to why this is: that the way you first see someone affects later perceptions because of expectation; that attractiveness is a central trait so we assume all the rest of the traits match; that we see people always as either 'good' or 'bad' rather than a mix of the two.

In summary, while a psychopath may disarm you with charm if they are also attractive it adds up to a dangerous combination as their good looks can lull others into a false sense of security. You need to be on your guard at those times when you do not have a great deal of information about someone – such as on first dates or at job interviews – as the 'halo effect' can make you overlook warning signs.

SUMMARY AND ADVICE

As if getting a date wasn't enough of a trial and tribulation, now you have psychopaths to worry about too. But dating is meant to be fun, so there are ways to protect yourself.

First of all – don't be too quick to judge. It takes psychologists several hours with various sources of information to work out to what degree someone is psychopathic, so you are not going to manage it in one date.

While online dating is a boon in our time-pressured lives, it is always better to meet someone 'in the real world' so you can see them in context, with friends, workmates or even family around them. In this case, take time to talk to the people who are with your potential date. In an article in *More* magazine (September 2010) titled 'Memoir: Dating A Psychopath', Chelsea Mitchell advises us to believe it if your date's mother doesn't like her own son. It's pretty telling, don't you think, if the people with them don't like them? 'I remembered that his mother had told me he was mean,' said Chelsea. 'I just thought that it was the ramblings of a sick old woman.'

If you are going to use a dating site, use an established one where members have to pay to subscribe; this protects your personal details and will have policies about inappropriate use. Make sure that you can 'block' people when you don't want to hear from them.

Observe the usual dating safety rules – meet in a public place, tell a friend where you are going, have your arrangements for getting there and back independently in place, have your mobile fully charged and with you, do not get drunk and don't leave your drink unattended.

Be suspicious of someone who has Too Much Information (TMI) syndrome, particularly if they are giving you a sob-story or telling you unlikely stories about their heroism. Ask yourself – does their story hold together or is it rife with inconsistencies?

By the same token, don't suffer from the TMI syndrome yourself. Dating is a gradual process of getting to know someone. You do not need to provide a first date with your address, entire life story and information about all your vulnerabilities (psychopaths will leap on this information but even if they are not psycho, you'll send them running anyway). It is great if your date is interested in you but be suspicious of anyone who appears to be fishing for financial or too-personal information.

Avoid treating the date like a job interview but remember that it is OK to ask questions about your date's friends, family, future plans and so on. Can he or she provide details about people and projects that they claim are important to them?

Finally, try not to be blinded by big romantic gestures and flattery on first dates. If someone appears just too good to be true . . . they might well be.

6

IS YOUR CHILD A PSYCHOPATH?

As parents we worry so much about doing the very best for our children and we want to believe that our loving them will be enough to bring out the best in them. So it can be bewildering and even frightening when our children behave badly, even if we understand that it is part of the normal developmental process for children to be naughty when toddlers and again as teenagers.

As they break away from parents, asserting their independence and exploring the world, both toddlers and teens typically test us with extreme selfish and reckless behaviours. But at what point should we become concerned that our child has crossed the threshold between what is normal and possibly psychopathic?

There is also the question of what 'good' parenting is. Bad parenting may seem obvious – neglect, abuse, exploitation – but hyper-parenting can breed narcissism. Is a psychopath born or created by the parents? Are there other external factors, such as exposure to onscreen violence or peer group dynamics, which could affect a child's potential psychopathy?

I was woken this morning – as I usually am – at the crack of dawn, to the sound of my son throwing his toys at his bedroom wall. Johnny is three years old but the 'terrible twos' have lasted for twenty months now. I brace myself for the long day ahead, go upstairs and see if today will be the day that Johnny wears the clothes I've picked out for him. Needless to say, it's not. Instead, after forty minutes of battling, he is wearing odd socks, his sister Maisie's Piglet slippers and a Superman costume, complete with flapping cape. He has worn this outfit every day for the last two months. Before that, he was Batman. I wouldn't mind so much but he's convinced he can fly when wearing it; despite the summer heat, all the windows have to be tightly locked shut or he'll try and jump out of them.

Breakfast is quick but not because Johnny is hungry. It's quick because no sooner have I put the bowl of cereal in front of him than he has thrown it onto the floor. He looks me right in the eye as he does this.

By this point I am already exhausted – and it's only 8 a.m. So I put him in a playpen and decide to try and send some emails. After twenty minutes, I am disturbed – by the eerie silence. Looking into his room, I see that Johnny is deeply involved in ripping apart my diary – page by page. I don't know how he got hold of it but before I can start to ask him any questions he sees me and, on cue, begins to howl then lie down flat, banging his head on the floor.

I thought perhaps the best thing would be to get out of the house and go to the supermarket. He was willing to get into his pushchair – but only after he had swapped the coat I had picked out for another.

Unfortunately, today at the supermarket was the day that they were doing a special promotion. On walking in, I spotted a woman handing out small pots of double-chocolate fudge ice-cream: the last thing my hyper Johnny needs. I tried to swerve out of her sight quickly but I was too late – he had seen her. The demand for ice-cream started in the fruit section and lasted all the way up to the bakery. His screams got louder and louder and the looks I was getting from the other shoppers were getting frostier and frostier. At the checkout he went quiet – because he was holding his breath. He went almost blue in the face until I finally caved in and went to get him some. When I looked up from the freezer compartment, Johnny was happily munching away on crisps, snatched from a blue-eyed little girl in an adjacent trolley. He put me in such a bad mood that I told him we wouldn't be going to the park today. He likes to be pushed higher and higher on the swings.

He reaches such a height I worry he's going to fall. Of course, when I told him this, his bottom lip started quivering and he started to cry. Which immediately made me feel like the worst mother in the world, so I did take him to the park.

When his father gets home, he'll ask Johnny what he did today and he'll say what he always says: 'I flew to the moon and back.' His father has learned not to contradict this version of the day's events by now.

I'd tell you more but frankly, I'm exhausted. Next week we are supposed to be going on holiday for a fortnight and the thought of the journey on the plane is already making me feel sick. I don't know if I can cope anymore.

Jenny, 36, exhausted mother

Should Jenny be worried that her son is displaying some of the classic traits of a psychopath? After all, psychopaths have to start somewhere, don't they? The Superman fantasies could be indicative of grandiosity; tearing up his mother's diary shows irresponsibility; the tantrums are a clear sign of poor anger controls; swapping coats at random is simple impulsivity; he needs extreme stimulation, as we see from his demands on the swing, and his tales of flying to the moon and back might be early signs of a pathological liar. But that doesn't mean that Johnny is showing signs of a lifelong dysfunction that could end with a twenty-five-year stretch in prison for murder, does it?

It could be that Johnny is simply a very ordinary toddler. This is most likely to be the case. While there has been some rather alarming research,[23] which suggests that psychopathic traits in adults can be traced back to their behaviour at three years old, it is always far better to assume that the 'problems' with your child are part and parcel of their natural development.

There are two stages in a child's emotional growth where 'psychopathic' features are to be expected, to some extent at least. Johnny is clearly in one of them. At two and three years old, children are beginning to develop their mental reasoning skills but are still largely egocentric and lack the ability to fully distinguish between fantasy and reality. They start to assert their independence but quickly become frustrated when they can't achieve their goals. Not being the most subtle of creatures at this point, this manifests itself in screaming tantrums, ruthless behaviour and some very strange choices.

The second stage of 'developmental psychopathy' is adolescence. Evolutionary psychologists describe this as a period of 'storm and stress'. It is a time when hormones, changing bodies and increasing levels of responsibility can conspire to turn previously delightful children into belligerent, inarticulate and sulky gremlins. Renowned psychologist Erik Erikson saw all teenagers as going through a stage of 'identity confusion' in which they are moody and obsessed with how they appear to others and experiment with a variety of behaviours which typically push against the boundaries placed on them by society.

WHEN BAD BRAINS HAPPEN TO GOOD TEENAGERS

Neuroscientists believe that, just as infants' brains undergo 'moulding' during the first years of life, some fundamental restructuring also takes place during adolescence.[24]

The parietal and frontal lobes, which are particularly associated with self-control, show a sudden growth surge between the ages of ten and twelve. This is followed by a dramatic shrinkage of synaptic connections throughout the teenage years. Just like pruning a tree, the brain appears to be disposing of superfluous matter and strengthening orderly processing paths.

This means that much of teenage behaviour may be to do with the brain being immature and in a developing state and not because they really, really, really hate you. (But then again, they might.)

So at what point do the behaviours tip over from being normal to deeply worrying?

We can look for the answer in the Youth Version of the Psychopathy Checklist, which is used with children aged between twelve and eighteen years old. This was developed because psychopathy has to start somewhere but children have less life experience and opportunity for acting out their psychopathic traits. So consideration needed to be given as to how to measure the core features according to how they might manifest in early life. According to this checklist, if a child sets fire to his bedroom for fun, frequently physically torments his younger sister, is overtly sexual with the younger girls at school and has been arrested fourteen times by the age of twelve ... then, yes, there is reason to worry. *If*, that is, you have been providing Johnny with a stable, loving family home, consistent discipline and he is not being abused – whether through bullying, neglect, physical violence or sexual abuse – by anyone in his world, whether that is your friends, his school or your wider family.

WHAT CAUSES PSYCHOPATHY?

Scientists have yet to provide us with a definitive answer as to whether psychopathy is caused by nature or nurture. In other words: is a psychopath created entirely genetically or is he a product of a faulty upbringing? Is it possible that a child born into a loving family can grow up displaying a large number of psychopathic traits? (Was Mrs Hitler a normal, affectionate mother?) Could it be that some parents can do little but stand back and watch aghast as their 'little angel' repeatedly violates their trust and love?

There are a number of schools of thought: that we are the product of our environment, or our genes or a combination of both. As we know, psychpaths over show various neuro-biological abnormalities (for example research measuring electrical activity in the brain of people who are asked to read and recognise words flashed up on a computer screen shows that 'normal' people respond to graphic words, like 'death' or 'rape', much quicker than neutral words. The brains of psychopaths make no distinction. But whether the differences between these brains are determined pre-birth or shaped during early childhood is almost impossible to determine.

There are certainly numerous psychopaths who did endure violent upbringings and who took on board lessons of aggression and abuse from their parents that they later re-enacted in violent crimes. But many, many more abused children do not go on to become psychopaths.

Hare's view is that 'psychopathy emerges from a complex – and poorly understood – interplay between biological factors and social forces'.[25] A combination of nature and nurture, in other words. A study has shown that while criminals from an unstable family background first appear in court at an average age of fifteen, those with a relatively stable background first appear in court at an average age of twenty-four. This suggests that those with dysfunctional families are more likely to begin a criminal career early. But this applies only to non-psychopathic criminals.

The psychopathic child begins a career of juvenile delinquency at an average age of fourteen *whether or not* they have a stable family background. In short, even if the psychopathic child has a loving family background he or she will still begin their criminal activity at a young age. (But Hare does acknowledge that psychopaths are affected by having unstable families in that those with a dysfunctional background are more likely to commit *violent* crimes.)

Hare is keen to stress that this does not let the parents off the hook altogether: 'Parenting behaviour may not be responsible for the essential ingredients of the disorder, but it may have a great deal to do with how the syndrome develops and is expressed.'

There is no question that children develop their conscience by observing their role models. In other words, if you want your son or daughter to learn the difference between right and wrong, *you* need to show them. Children need reliable experience from which to learn and it is the presence of harsh and inconsistent discipline which comes up time and again in psychopathy literature.

THE CAMBRIDGE STUDY IN DELINQUENT DEVELOPMENT

This is one of the longest ever studies into criminal behaviour, following 411 males from the ages of around eight to forty-eight years old. The children were chosen from working class inner city areas in South London in 1961 and were assessed several times over the course of their adult years. The aims of this project were to look at the factors contributing to juvenile offending and the subsequent development, or not, of a lifetime of crime.

The study found that over half the sample broke the law at some point, with criminal activity peaking at the age of seventeen. But those who began their conviction careers at the earliest age tended to commit the most offences and to continue their offending far longer into adulthood. Those who found themselves in the dock between the ages of 10 and 16 committed 77 per cent of all the crimes recorded in the study. Seven per cent of this group were 'chronic offenders' who were responsible for half of all the crimes counted and carried on adding to their criminal record until well into their fourth decades. So, the study supports the suggestion that it is fairly normal for teenagers to get into trouble with the law, just not persistently or at a very young age.

On average the conviction careers of the chronic offenders lasted from the ages of 14 to 35. Criminal activity, on average across the sample – i.e. for the average, non-psychopathic teenager – peaked at the age of 17. So the ordinary teenager may shoplift or try to break into a car and other such petty crimes but they will start to grow out of it after the age of 17. Whereas the more serious, possibly psychopathic, criminal will continue to engage in law-breaking activity for another couple of decades, after which time it will taper off. This may be because they are in prison, or because they mellow or because they tire of the criminal life.

The project also found that it was possible to predict which children would become career criminals from risk factors present when they were between just 8 and 10 years old. These were:

- Poor educational achievement.

- Family poverty and deprivation; a large family size with low income and poor housing.

- Parents using harsh, authoritarian parenting practices, poor supervision of the children or long periods of separation.

- Hyper-activity, poor concentration, restlessness, risk taking and impulsive behaviour.

- Disruptive school behaviour, including dishonesty and aggression.

- Parents have convictions and/or the presence of delinquent siblings.

THE SEVEN SIGNS OF THE PSYCHOPATHIC CHILD

Let's study two brothers, both teenagers, for those signs that tip the balance between normal and psychopathic.

Tom and Peter are twins, born just minutes apart. But right from the off, they were different. Where Tom was a placid, smiling baby, Peter was a screamer. They were, however, quite close as young children and, egged on by Peter, Tom would often be encouraged to take part in naughty pranks that would drive their parents to distraction.

At least, that was how it looked. Because Tom may have looked as if butter wouldn't melt in his mouth but he wasn't always innocent (there were complaints from the school about his disruptive behaviour and there was a nasty incident when the neighbours accused him of setting fire to their shed). And Peter, despite his constantly dirty knees and face, wasn't always guilty. In fact, when they both became teenagers, their parents started to wonder: who was good and who was bad?

When they turned fifteen, Peter could most often be found in front of the mirror, picking at his spots, re-combing his hair and mentally trying to will his stubble to grow. Despite repeated banging on the bathroom door every morning by his exasperated brother and parents, Peter doesn't come out until *he* is ready.

Tom, on the other hand, is brashly confident of his looks and brags frequently about how he has the prettiest girl in the school in the palm of his hand. Despite his failing grades, he is unconcerned about the future, explaining to anyone who asks that he is going to do 'something big in the City' and become a millionaire by the time he is twenty-one. When teachers ask where his homework is, Tom likes to just shrug and answer that the question set 'bored' him – could they ask him to do something more challenging next time?

Sign I Peter is displaying frustrating but nonetheless typical signs of teenage self-obsession; the average adolescent isn't only sensitive to, but is generally quite critical of, his or her changing appearance. No such anxieties for Tom, and his self-assurance appears to have tipped over into a misplaced grandiosity, the psychopathic trait of excessive self-regard.

One Saturday, Tom and Peter take two girls to the fairground for a double date. They go on all the rides but Peter insists on taking his date several times on the Ginormous Double Dipper Freak Ride. She is green by the third go and seriously in danger of throwing up her candy floss by the fifth, but Peter thinks this is hilarious and continues to buy more tickets and insist that she stops being 'boring'.

Tom, meanwhile, has got bored of the dipper and taken his date off to the Ghost Train. She thinks this is pretty childish and isn't at all impressed but Tom puts something in her mouth just as they set off . . . it's an Ecstasy tablet. Tom has taken two. As soon as she realises, she is terrified but Tom merely laughs. There's nothing to worry about, he tells her, he's done them loads of times and if she wants to calm down he'll roll them both a joint to help.

Sign 2 All teenagers seek thrills and while Peter is being selfish in dragging his poor, vomiting date on a cheap ride over and over again – he's only being a typical teen. They believe at that age that they are invincible (as they do as toddlers – it's a natural need for courage to explore the world around them). Tom's drug use, however, could indicate something much darker at work – particularly as he forces it on his date. His parents need to watch out for continuing, excessive drug use, particularly if combined with other activities such as driving fast cars before he's even got his licence, riding his skateboard down the middle of a busy road and challenging burly bouncers to fights. Psychopaths are, remember, stimulation-seeking creatures and drug abuse is common in teen-psychos because it is a cheap and easily available way to meet needs for stimulation.

Tom is a source of bewilderment to his parents, particularly as he seems to lie constantly, often for no apparent reason: that it wasn't him who finished the cereal and put the empty box back in the cupboard; that he was asleep when the postman rang the bell; that he had fed the dog as asked; that the drugs in his room were planted there by Peter. But Peter lies too – about staying with his friend Sam when his parents are sure that he is sleeping overnight with a new girlfriend: if he is having sex with her, that's illegal as she is under-age.

Sign 3 On the face of it, Peter's lies are more serious – but most teenage boys want to keep their private lives private and are well practised in keeping the truth about their sexual activities from their parents. In fact, it is Tom's constant lies that should give rise for more concern, particularly the fact that he lies for no real gain – simply for the kick of it.

WHEN TELLING LIES IS A GOOD SIGN

An article in *The Sunday Times* carried the headline: 'Trust me, telling fibs is a sure sign of success'.[26] The piece reported on research carried out by Dr Kang Lee at the Institute of Child Study at the University of Toronto on 1,200 children, in which they were left in a room and asked not to look at the toy behind them (which of course they did). The children were later asked if they had done as they were told. Dr Lee concluded that many of the children had learnt to tell a lie showed they had reached an important step in their mental development. The children with the best cognitive abilities could tell the best lies, showing they had developed 'executive functioning', which includes them being able to keep the truth at the back of their mind so that their lie sounds more convincing.

At the age of two, 20 per cent of children will lie, rising to 50 per cent by three and almost 90 per cent at four. This trend peaks at the age of twelve, when almost all children lie (but not all of the time) and is back down to 70 per cent by the age of sixteen. (To compare this with adults, a study commissioned by the Science Museum found that the average male tells around 1,092 lies a year.) The researchers said there is 'no link' between telling occasional fibs in childhood and any later tendency to cheat in exams or become a con-artist as an adult. Nor did strict parenting have any influence.

On a typical Friday night, Tom and Peter's parents find themselves exhausted by both their sons' anger. Peter has come home two hours after curfew and, when confronted by his dad, storms upstairs, banging every door he goes through and shouting, 'You don't understand!'

Tom staggers in hiding bloodied knuckles – he has been brought back by the police several times, having been in the middle of a pub brawl that spilled out into the street. Tom is always unrepentant – each time it is, inevitably, someone else's fault for having looked at him funny, chatted up his girlfriend or spilled a drink on his jeans. However, it was harder when he had to explain one night that he'd punched a policeman. If his parents try to argue that he cannot possibly always be innocent, Tom punches the nearest wall and cries out in pain, 'Look what you made me do!'

Sign 4 Peter's outbursts of anger are merely symptomatic of being a frustrated teenager, keen to assert his independence and break away from his parents. But Tom displays the psychopathic quality of frequent and excessive loss of temper – he is unable to resist flaring up into violence at the slightest provocation.

All of this would be bearable, think the parents, if they had a sense of their boys preparing for life in the outside world and making plans to do well. While their friends' children are busy setting up work experience in the summer holidays, Peter sleeps in until noon and only gets up to spend several hours on his beloved Facebook. Tom, meanwhile, for all his talk of being a millionaire by the age of twenty-one, has been bunking off school and didn't even turn up for some of his GCSE exams.

Sign 5 Just when teenagers ought to be embracing the excitement that life offers the youthful and energetic, they seem to spend all their time sleeping or staring at a computer. No wonder the parents go mad. But Peter is only playing to type for a boy of his age; studies have shown that teenagers' body clocks are set at different times to children and adults, making them stay up later and sleep in longer.[27] Tom, however, is showing a more worrying symptom – a lack of any realistic goals. While he may talk vaguely of being a millionaire, he has no plan as to how he is going to do this or even the inclination to help himself by getting qualifications first. A psychopath believes that he can just 'wing it' through life and that he'll get what he wants – even if he doesn't really know what that is.

Only last week, the twins' parents were frantic with worry when Peter's teachers telephoned to say that he hadn't turned up for school that day – where was he? When he still wasn't back at midnight, they were on the verge of calling the police. Just then they got a call from him – he'd decided to go to a concert three hours' away to see his favourite band. They were furious, but at least he was safe.

But their relief was short-lived when, on the Monday, Tom came home to announce that not only had he dumped his new best friend, he was also quitting school. 'The school has nothing to teach me,' he declared. He tells them he is going to go 'into business', even though he has been sacked from his last three Saturday jobs for non-attendance.

Sign 6 What teenager hasn't bunked off to spend a day with his mates or follow a band to the ends of the earth (or at least the end of the train line)? It's practically a rite of passage. But while Peter's parents might feel more vulnerable when their son is apparently missing until late at night, they should be more focused on Tom's spur-of-the-moment actions, whereby he will break off plans, relationships and commitments merely because he feels like it.

Against what seem like overwhelming odds at times, Tom and Peter's parents try to instil in their children a sense of responsibility. They feel that they have failed. Peter's second hamster has just died after a mere four months in his care. Either through dehydration or possibly the marijuana 'blow backs' that Peter thought would be 'funny' to inflict on the

117

tiny creature. Tom, meanwhile, appears to have killed the dog. This occurred when his 'experiment' failed. Of course, no dachshund could survive leaping after a ball deliberately thrown out of a third-floor window. Little do his parents (or the neighbours) know, but previous four-legged experiments are buried in the back garden.

Sign 7 Peter's failure to look after his hamster is not something to be dismissed and it's certainly clear by now that even by comparison with Tom, Peter is no golden boy. But Tom's treatment of family pets shows a breathtaking callousness. Sadistic treatment of animals is one of the clearest possible warning signs of possible psychopathy and should indicate to Tom's parents that it is time to seek professional advice.

WHEN IS YOUR CHILD BEING NAUGHTY AND WHEN IS IT SOMETHING MORE?

1. When you pick up George, four, from his first day of school, the teacher asks to have a quiet word with you. She says:

    A) George had to be put in the corner after repeatedly getting into fights and biting the other boys.

    B) George had to be put in the corner after repeatedly chasing the girls and trying to kiss them, which made them cry.

    C) George had to be put in the corner after pouring glue into the sandbox, while the other children were still in it.

2. It's the morning of your sister's wedding and your daughter Maisie, six, is lined up to be the bridesmaid. But at 8 a.m. you find her:

A) Hiding in the cupboard under the stairs — she doesn't like the thought of all those people staring at her in the church.

B) Cutting up her bridesmaid's dress into tiny pieces — at least she's only got as far as the left sleeve.

C) Waking up your sister by asking her if she, too, saw 'uncle' kissing Jenny from over the road last week?

3. **Michael, eight, has been very quiet in his bedroom all morning. You should be enjoying the peace and quiet but instead you know that:**

A) Michael is most likely to be tormenting the hamster by poking the poor beast awake, gelling its hair into a Mohican and encouraging it to fight his Ninja Turtle action-figure.

B) Michael is most likely to be playing forbidden violent games on his brother's computer, which he has hacked into while the teenager is still asleep.

C) Michael is most likely to be found performing 'open heart surgery' on his younger sister's cuddly toys as a surprise for when she gets back from ballet.

4. **It's your birthday and Susan, twelve, has promised you a treat. You take advantage of a lie-in and wait expectantly.**

A) Susan brings you up breakfast in bed — it consists of a packet of crisps and a tall glass of vodka.

B) Susan creeps out of the back door and doesn't come home until 6 p.m.

C) Susan sleeps in longer. When she finally gets up at noon and you ask about your treat, she merely grunts and goes back to her room.

5.   You wonder if you should be worried because after he comes home from school, Tim, thirteen, goes straight to his room and doesn't come down again except to fetch a plate of supper. This is what he's doing:

A) Listening to The Grateful Dead albums back to back at full volume (and sometimes backwards, just to see if they really do contain Satanic messages).

B) Playing Mash 'Em Up computer games non-stop.

C) Looking at *Monster Jugs* magazine (you found it hidden under his mattress).

6.   You are thrilled – John, fifteen, has been made captain of the football team at school. But the joy is short-lived because:

A) The sports teacher calls you at home to explain that John has had his captaincy removed after he was found naked in the showers with a girl from his class.

B) The sports teacher calls you at home to explain that John has had his captaincy removed after he was caught throwing matches – his mates were running betting sweepstakes.

C) John fails to show up for his first match as captain – he's on a train on his way to see his girlfriend instead.

7.   It's a Friday night and at 11 p.m. your doorbell rings. It's a policeman with your son Mark, sixteen. Before the copper can start to explain, you tell him to be quiet. You already know what it's about – it's happened almost every Friday for the last six months.

A) Mark has been caught in the local pub trying to flog the family television set.

B) Mark has been caught in the local pub trying to buy marijuana.

C) Mark has been thrown out of the local pub and has been found semi-conscious surrounded by cans of lager in the local park.

8. **Saturday night looms. You try to encourage your daughter Lucie, seventeen, to stay in and watch *The X Factor* with you. But you know what she really wants to do:**

A) Hang out with her friends on the estate, throwing stones at passing cars and getting drunk on vodka and Red Bull.

B) Hang out with her friends on the estate and have sex in the broken down lift with a local spotty boy.

C) Hang out with her friends on the estate until the police break up the inevitable fight.

9. **You tell Simon, eighteen, that he will not be allowed to spend a week in the Costa del Sol on holiday with his friends after his A levels. It's too expensive and too risky. He shouts:**

A) 'I hate you. I wish you were dead.'

B) 'I'm going anyway. You can't stop me.'

C) 'I'm going to make you regret this. Just you wait and f***ing see.'

10. **It's New Year's Eve and, having taken everyone on holiday, you are hoping that at midnight all your family will be gathered around you. Instead:**

A) The teenagers are passed out by 10 p.m. having stolen a bottle of tequila and got started on it that afternoon.

B) The teenagers have gone to the beach for a bonfire party and are refusing to come and join in the family celebration.

C) The teenagers are in the local nightclub.

Answers:

Whatever you've ticked, they are certainly very naughty. But however much you may wish you could be sure of getting them locked up and throwing away the key, they are not psychopathic. They're just normal children. Don't worry – it may last almost twenty years but it's just a passing phase . . .

The more disturbing signs that could indicate psychopathic behaviour include thefts from other children and parents; vandalism and fire-setting; hurting or killing animals; bullying; very early sexual and extreme experimentation, particularly if coercing other children; truanting from home and school; failing to respond to reprimands and punishment. Do remember that psychopaths show a cluster of behaviours so you shouldn't panic at one or two isolated incidents.

HOW ADHD CAN BE MISTAKEN FOR PSYCHOPATHY

Studies show a high 'co-morbidity' between psychopathic tendencies and Attention Deficit Hyperactivity Disorder (ADHD) i.e. they are often found together.[28] ADHD can be found in up to as many as 75 per cent of cases of psychopathic children.[29]

The link between the two is far from clear and there are many factors involved that need to be explored further. British scientists have very recently discovered, from looking at DNA segments, the first direct genetic link to ADHD. This new knowledge claims that children with the condition are likely to have small but important segments of DNA that are either missing or duplicated in their genome.[30] Nothing similar has yet to be established for psychopaths. And it seems that the type of brain dysfunction found in psychopaths is quite different to that associated with ADHD: psychopathy is associated with amygdala dysfunction but this is not seen in those with ADHD.[31]

There is a danger that teenagers with ADHD can be mislabelled by psychiatrists, as well as teachers and parents, as psychopathic for their persistent 'naughtiness' as some of the behavioural manifestations of the two disorders can appear similar. Children with ADHD may do poorly at school and be rejected by their peers because they are inappropriate in their play and in the way they interact with their classmates. Being disruptive and generally different marks these children out and can cause strain at home, too, with parents feeling at the end of their tethers. This can lead to parents either giving up on the child, or being inconsistent or too harsh when it comes to discipline. Consequently, an ADHD teenager may identify with kids who have similar difficulties – in other words, the 'wrong crowd', and so risk falling into juvenile delinquency.

REWARDS AND PUNISHMENT DON'T WORK

All children need to be provided with clear and reliable discipline, but a child who is higher risk for the development of psychopathy requires an unswerving approach to give them the best chance of grasping the difference between right and wrong. The psychological term 'passive avoidance' refers to children learning to respond to things that will be rewarding, while also learning to avoid those things that will punish them. For example, you learn quickly as a child that saying 'please' will get you ice-cream and biting your mother on the leg will get you sent to your room.

At least, most children will learn. As we have already learnt, psychopaths are exceptionally poor at learning from punishment or reward. So poor, in fact, that 'passive avoidance errors' are made even when money or cigarettes are offered as incentives to learn.[32] A child who is repeatedly misbehaving despite being sent to the naughty step or promised sweets to stop could be a psychopath in the making. It's not that the child sometimes responds but that they *never* respond; it's a repeated inability to learn that sets them apart from others.

IS TECHNOLOGY TURNING US INTO PSYCHOPATHS?

Daniel Petric is a US teenager who shot his parents in the head for taking away his games console. He wanted to play Halo 3, a first-person shooter game. Daniel was just sixteen years old at the time of his crime; his father was a preacher. When questioned by police, he initially told them that his father had shot his mother, before turning the gun on himself (the father survived and, together with forensic evidence, contradicted Daniel's version of events).

Before shooting his parents, Daniel came up behind them and said, 'Would you guys close your eyes? I have a surprise for you.' When he fled the scene, he took the game with him.

The game was extensively quoted in the evidence as it had been locked away in a safe with the 9mm handgun that Daniel used to shoot his parents. The case generated intense debate about the nature of video game addiction (it was said that Daniel played Halo 3 for eighteen hours at a time). The defence claimed that – among other things – Daniel had diminished responsibility because he had played the game so much he didn't understand the finality of shooting his parents. He was sentenced to prison for twenty-three years and will be eligible for parole in 2031.

Before we go blaming the video game industry for Daniel's matricide, there is no link between technology and psychopathy. There isn't really a conclusive link between violent video games and serious violence in children or adults but it *is* possible that they raise our 'violence thresholds' by desensitising us to extreme acts, and rewarding us for them – after all, these games reward acts such as killing and therefore make people already prone to knee-jerk aggressive behaviour even more so.

Children will often mimic what they see on screen. So do you really want them to spend hours in front of a killing game? In cases where graphics are particularly realistic children are more likely to get muddled between what is fantasy and what is reality. Computer games in the twenty-first century are, after all, light years away from the antics of *Tom & Jerry* cartoons. Sexually graphic and violent films, video games and so on have an age-restriction certificate for a reason – pay attention to them!

There is a reasonably well-established link between video game play, too much time spent in front of inappropriately adult TV and bullying.[33] Researchers looked at six-to-eleven-year-olds and found that those who were observed to be playground bullies watched more television than non-bullies (an average of five hours a day). They do not say, or were unable to state, exactly what the causal links are.

There are elements of game playing that research has suggested can support child cognitive and motor development and even general wellbeing.[34] Appropriate video games with an educational theme that encourage thinking and creativity rather than speed, and those that have a pro-social message, have positive qualities.

My advice would be to treat all media much in the same way as sweets. Don't allow your children a constant diet of it, but in moderation it is fine. Most children spend 7.7 hours a week playing video games and a staggering 32.1 in front of the TV.[35] This is not a healthy amount of time to spend on this activity: around two hours a day watching television is the most a child should spend. If you are worried about the amount of time your child spends in front of a screen of some kind, you will find useful information in *The Media Diet for Kids* by Teresa Orange and Louise O'Flynn.[36]

THE PHENOMENA OF TEENAGE KILLERS

In 1999, Eric Harris, aged eighteen, and Dylan Klebold, seventeen, walked into their school, Columbine High, and shot dead thirteen people and injured twenty-three more before taking their own lives. They had been planning their attack for over a year. With an alarming number of similar cases in the USA and across the world (between 1996 and the time of going to press there have been a total of forty-eight shooting incidents by students worldwide), parents now fear this type of crime emerging in the UK. The event opened up debate about the impact of school sub-cultures and the 'in' or 'out' cliques. Harris and Klebold were unpopular 'Goths'.

Teenage murderers are invariably described in the media as 'loners' but a study by the US Secret Service found that there isn't a specific 'type' – some were described as having friends and even coming from the 'ideal, all-American family'.[37]

They do have some features in common, however. Primarily they tend to be male: there have been only two known incidents of female teenage killers – one led to the song 'I Don't Like Mondays' by the Boomtown Rats after lead singer Bob Geldof heard about sixteen-year-old Brenda Ann Spencer. She killed two adults and injured eight children and a police officer in a playground in California, giving as her explanation, 'I don't like Mondays; this livens up the day.' They also all share a feeling of being ostracised by their peers. Investigating the Columbine incident, the FBI concluded that Harris in particular had masterminded the massacre and was a psychopath who had a 'messianic level superiority complex'; Klebold had gone along with it while suffering from depression.[38]

As gun crime increases around the world, parents need to be mindful of any behavioural displays in their children that could indicate their potential to commit such awful crime. The FBI have written a paper on how to assess threats made by pupils.[39] They emphasise that their list of indicators is not in any way predictive and any assessment should not rest on one or two isolated incidents or 'one bad day' in a child's life. Someone who carries out a violent activity such as a school shooting will have displayed a pattern of behaviours both at home and at school, just as we have emphasised in this book that a psychopath is only someone who has displayed a cluster of psychopathic traits.

There are several areas that they recommend parents and teachers look at when assessing whether a teenager's threat of violence is one likely to be carried out. These range from school and social and family dynamics to the child's personality, but 'leakage' is considered to be one of the most important clues to precede a student's violent act. Leakage is when a student – intentionally or otherwise – reveals clues to feelings, thoughts, fantasies, attitudes or intentions to signal a violent act, whether in the form of subtle threats, boasts, innuendos or ultimatums. These might occur in diaries, songs, poetry, doodles, tattoos or videos. They may even be dismissed by the student immediately after they are expressed as 'nothing'. But they could be a cry for help, a sign of inner conflict or even a boast that might appear to be empty but is in fact a real threat.

This should all be kept in perspective: the actual threat of a school shooting is very low statistically. In assessing whether it is likely to happen, a school and its parents need to ensure that they are always appraised of a child's life in the round – at home, with friends and at school. As the paper concludes, 'violent behaviour develops progressively', and so it is down to the adults around the child to monitor observable signs in the evolutionary process of the aggression.

THE STORY OF BRIAN BLACKWELL – THE 'PERFECT SON' TURNED KILLER

On the 5 September 2004, in Liverpool, two policemen responded to a call from a neighbour of the Blackwell family. He had noticed a strong smell coming from the house and when he investigated further he found the windows 'caked' in flies. Although the neighbour had not seen Mr and Mrs Blackwell for weeks, he had spotted their son Brian recently leaving the premises.

Inside, the police found the bodies of Sydney Blackwell, seventy-one, and his wife Jacqueline, sixty, in advanced stages of decomposition. Both had suffered multiple and brutal injuries.

Their son Brian, eighteen, was quickly found at his girl-friend's house. He said he had last seen his parents on 23 July, when he went to America on holiday and that he had returned to the house only twice since: on 10 August to pick up keys to the car from the garage and 'two or three days' before, when he collected post from the porch. He was immediately cautioned and arrested on suspicion of his parents' murder. Brian was later jailed for life, having pleaded guilty to manslaughter on the grounds of diminished responsibility. In July 2011 he will be considered for release but the judge at the time of sentencing said that 'The present evidence suggests that the conclusion [that Brian is no longer a threat to society] is unlikely to ever be reached.'

For those who knew the Blackwell family, the news was shocking. Brian had been a model pupil – winning art prizes, a scholarship to a private school and all As in his GCSEs – and he had provisional offers to study medicine at Nottingham and Edinburgh universities. He was even a decent competitive tennis player, with a minor sponsorship from an Austrian firm.

But when we look a little closer, Brian was not so picture perfect after all. From an early age, he appears to have become accustomed to lying. First of all to his fellow pupils about his SATS results. He had few friends in his new senior school and ate alone in the library for the first two years. At fifteen he started to 'tag along' with a group, but those who knew him described him as 'arrogant', 'quite cocky' and 'a liar or more of an exaggerator'.

When Brian got his first girlfriend at the start of 2004, the exaggerations stepped right up into more extreme lies. He told her that Nike UK sponsored him, to the tune of £79,000 a year. He said that he had some prize money from his tennis matches and wished to buy a Porsche or Mercedes; he even took his girlfriend to a dealership.

Not long afterwards he promised to buy his girlfriend a car. Then he told her that she could work for him as his manager or personal secretary and that this would be paid for by Nike. The wages would be £82,500 with a £20,000 bonus and expenses up to £96,000. He even showed her apparent emails and documents from Nike, gave her an application form to complete and got her to sign a fifty-five-page contract.

Brian then wrote a cheque for £39,000, which was supposed to be three months' salary. When the cheque bounced – twice – Brian blamed this on his mother 'preying on his account'. In fact, he had put a stop on the cheque: he was 9 pence overdrawn.

In May of that year, Brian put a £100 deposit on a Ford Ka costing £6,600. He applied to banks for account upgrades and credit cards, saying he was 'a semi-professional tennis player' and 'about to play in the French Open Tennis championships'. He even managed to withdraw £9,000 from the fixed-rate bond set up for his university years, saying that his father had died. His father, at that point at least, was very much alive.

Brian bought his girlfriend the car, an extra alongside the – allegedly expensive – jewellery he had been showering on her. Later, she discovered the jewellery was all cheap imitation. Still, he did get her Dior T-shirts, a Dior handbag, flowers . . .

By early July, Brian told her that he'd bought a Mercedes SL 350 for £60,000 and it was parked up at a flat he'd bought for £450,000. He also asked her to come to America with him as he was playing in a tennis tournament there. On 24 and 25 July several expensive flights were booked – from Manchester to New York (business class), New York to Miami, Miami to San Francisco and finally back to London Heathrow. All were paid for using his parents' credit cards.

On the night that he killed his parents, Brian burned his bloodstained clothing in the chiminea in the garden. He then booked a taxi just after midnight to his girlfriend's house and made a show of 'saying goodbye' to the folks indoors. The next day, the two of them went on their luxurious holiday. When they got back, he stayed at his girlfriend's house, explaining that his parents had gone to Spain and he had lost his keys. In reality, he had returned to the house containing the bloodied dead bodies of his parents in order to pick up belongings and continue to apply for credit in their names. All this, without giving away any telltale signs that something was terribly wrong.

On 19 August Brian got his A level results: four As. He complained to school friends that he was disappointed with his parents for not 'coming home' to celebrate his big day.

Following debate by five psychiatric experts prior to his trial it was accepted that Brian was 'a very abnormal young man' and certainly demonstrated tendencies very highly indicative of psychopathy. The judge described him as 'an arch deceiver, an accomplished and resourceful liar and highly manipulative'. However, given his preoccupation with fantasies of himself as the rich and successful 'sportsman', a diagnosis of Narcissistic Personality Disorder was considered more appropriate. The court accepted that the killings were probably committed during a 'narcissistic rage' when his parents objected to his outrageous holiday plans.

In the next chapter we will revisit Brian's case to ask if perhaps genetic influences or the way he was parented contributed to his extreme behaviours.

THE RUSSIAN BOY SENT BACK HOME ON A ONE-WAY TICKET

In March 2010, a thirty-three-year-old unmarried nurse called Torry Hansen from Tennessee, USA, put a seven-year-old Russian boy she had adopted six months previously on a ten-hour flight back to Moscow with a note that read: 'After giving my best to this child, I am sorry to say that for the safety of my family, friends, and myself, I no longer wish to parent this child.' He arrived alone where a man, who had been paid $200 by the family, picked him up and dropped him off at the Russian education ministry.

Torry did not tell the boy she was rejecting him but told

him he was going on an 'excursion' to Moscow. Torry and her mother, Nancy, claimed the little boy, Artem Saveliev, had 'violent episodes', which culminated in a threat to burn the family's home to the ground. 'He drew a picture of our house burning down, and he'll tell anybody that he's going to burn our house down with us in it,' said the grandmother. 'It got to be where you feared for your safety. It was terrible.'

In the letter, addressed to 'Whom It May Concern', Torry added: 'This child is mentally unstable. He is violent and has severe psychopathic issues/behaviours. I was lied to and misled by the Russian Orphanage workers and director regarding his mental stability and other issues.'

In September of the previous year, Torry had spent four days observing Artem in the Vladivostock orphanage, where he had been placed at the age of six when his natural mother, an alcoholic, had been forced to give him up. Torry renamed him Justin Hansen and took him back to the US to be a new brother to her son, Logan.

Of his 'psychopathic issues/behaviours', Torry chronicled a list of problems: hitting, screaming, spitting at her and threatening to kill family members. These episodes were often sparked when he was denied something he wanted, such as toys or video games.

For his part, once back in Russian care, Artem spoke of a grandmother who shouted at him and a mother who did not love him and who had dragged him by the hair. He had, however, got on well with his brother Logan. So – is this a child with psychopathic tendencies or not?

My money, for what it is worth, is not on the child. This is a case of a small boy from a poor part of Russia, who had been raised by a young alcoholic mother (she was nineteen when he was born), unable to cope with him. The neglect and suffering that he may have gone through before being taken into care might have been severely damaging to his emotional development. He was then placed in an orphanage before being taken thousands of miles away from anyone he knew and from any recognisable cultural reference point. (Torry learnt 'a few Russian words' to talk to him but one can only imagine that his daily life otherwise was very American and not what he was used to.) He even had to answer to a different name.

Spitting, kicking, biting and 'threatening' to burn the house down are not pleasant behaviours to see in a child but they are not necessarily psychopathic. They could also be the actions of a bewildered, frustrated and unhappy young boy.

A child's environment is of supreme importance, as is constancy. Despite the fact that children go through big changes during their early childhood and in their teens, as outlined earlier, it doesn't mean that they can readily adopt and adapt to all change.

This case came in the wake of the deaths of three Russian children adopted by Americans and it caused the Russian authorities to put a freeze on any further adoptions. No doubt there have been many more successful adoptions with loving parents, but the sad story of Artem and the Hansens only illustrates that children rarely mould perfectly to your expectations, particularly the unrealistic ones.

SUMMARY AND ADVICE

Given that psychopathy is most likely to be the result of a combination of factors – genetics, neurobiological differences, parenting – it's probably best that you focus on the one you can control: how you parent your child.

- Children learn from those around them: it should go without saying that it is never acceptable to expose a child to physical, emotional or verbal abuse, even if it is not directly aimed at them. A child who witnesses adults treating each other badly will grow up believing that other people's intentions are malevolent and it is a 'dog eat dog' world.

- Under no circumstances label your child a psychopath. If your child presents a range of problem behaviours that you are convinced are beyond what might reasonably expected given their age and environment, visit your GP in order to access the correct assessment and support.

- Be wary of becoming overly negative in your interpretations of child behaviour. Remember that younger children lack the sophistication to fully appreciate how their naughty behaviour impacts upon others. Older children can also be in a strangely blinkered place when experiencing huge physical or emotional adjustments, particularly in their teenage years when hormones surge. If you provide children with the constant message that they are nasty, wilful or disobedient, they will absorb this and have little incentive to behave differently. Even when children are at their most infuriating, parents need to maintain expressions of warmth: ideally, there should be twenty positive, praising or affectionate interactions to every negative one.

- Be as consistent as possible in the way in which you (in partnership with any other adult members of your household) manage naughty behaviour. The most effective disciplinary style is confident, firm but fair, as opposed to austere authoritarian or weakly permissive extremes.

- Your home needs clear rules and boundaries but these should be prescriptive rather than proscriptive – i.e. detail what your child 'should do' rather than 'must not do'. This type of guidance has been found to make children more generous. It is also helpful to encourage children to contribute to the rule setting, so that they understand the reasoning behind them and are therefore more likely to stick to them.

- Try to engender a sense of community in your child. Some school programmes incorporate elements of community voluntary work, animal care, older children teaching younger children, role-play and encouraging children to speak up about bullying so that they are not just passive bystanders when 'bad' things are happening. On the whole, these projects – compared to more traditional regimes – produce children who are more empathetic and tolerant of others, less prone to prejudice and stereotyping and even like school more. [40] You can discuss these opportunities with your child's school or provide similar yourself. Take the time to teach children about different groups of people – introduce them to diverse mix of ethnicity, age, gender and ability and allow for open discussion of these differences. Insist that they notice and take account of other people when making decisions. Teach kids how to negotiate and compromise, and ensure that they see kind, caring and cooperative behaviour modelled by you.

- A surprising thing for many parents may be realising that hyper-parenting – when mum and dad oversee every tiny detail of their child's life and encourage them to believe that they are the 'best' in every way – can be as damaging as neglect. What you may see as good parenting, looking after a child's interests and trying to secure their future success, can engender a dangerous level of narcissism. Bad parenting is not as simple as leaving your child to their own devices. In fact, occasionally that would be a good thing!

- Sandy Hotchkiss, in *Why Is It Always About You?* suggests that parents try to recognise and encourage their child's specific skills, rather than mindlessly repeating 'You can do it!' to someone who clearly can't. Furthermore, they should encourage a grounded and realistic sense of their place in the world – for example, if they enjoy major sporting success, send them out to do charity work. And although you may feel that your little darling is far more interesting than anyone else, you should prevent them from dominating in groups. This will stop them from becoming stuck in the centre of their own narrow universe.

- Children must be given the space to break away from parental influence and be allowed to experiment. A child who is hampered by overly rigid safeguards and expectations may develop a 'negative identity' – one that is borne only out of a desire not to do what the world expects of them. Teenagers in particular need to break away from parents in order to assert themselves as independent beings: it is healthy that they should rebel against their parents at some point. Teenagers who are expected to conform to a set of very hard-and-fast rules may very probably react in a corresponding fashion, rebelling with equal strength and breaking as many rules as possible. Not to mention that a less anxious teen may feel that if one rule is broken and they are going to be in trouble, they may as well break them all – an 'in for a penny, in for a pound' rationale.

7

IS YOUR PARENT A PSYCHOPATH?

Your parents are the most significant figures in the early years of your life. They are certainly the most likely to influence your attitude towards life and how you carry yourself within it. Their decisions on the clothes you wear as a child, the food you eat, the school you go to and the friends you see will have a lasting impact. Many people, as adults, will attribute their general sense of wellbeing – or otherwise – to their parents.

A psychopathic parent will either neglect their child or view the child as an extension of themselves, placing unbearable pressure on them to behave in the 'correct' way.

The nature vs nurture debate still rages and nowhere more vehemently than when discussing psychopaths. But one thing is clear: even if a psychopath is born psychopathic, their upbringing dictates the manner in which the problem manifests.

To the outside world, Christina was the luckiest girl on earth. As a tiny blonde baby she was adopted by one of Hollywood's biggest stars and consequently given a life most can only dream of: a huge house, lavish birthday parties, famous friends and a wardrobe full of dresses fit for a little princess. Yet, the truth was as different as a movie set is from real life. Christina's mother, Joan, was prone to sudden, irra-tional outbursts of anger and over the years a catalogue of incidents built up that eventually meant mother and daughter barely spoke.

After suffering seven miscarriages and a divorce, Joan had decided to adopt. Christina's babyhood was idyllic; the trouble started when, as a growing girl, she started to show signs of an independent will. As a young girl of four, having had a year of swimming lessons, Christina was eager to show off to her mother. They raced the width of the pool and her mother let her win. So then they raced the length of the pool, several times, each time her mother beating her easily. Christina was furious but her mother just laughed: 'Christina, I could have won all the time. I'm bigger than you are. I'm faster than you are. I can win all the time.'

On another day, as punishment for ripping tiny little pieces out of the wallpaper by her bed, Joan took a pair of scissors and shredded the four-year-old Christina's favourite yellow dress. She was then ordered to wear it for a week and if anyone asked her why she was wearing a dress in tatters, she was to reply, 'I don't like pretty things.'

Throughout her childhood, Christina lived in fear of 'night raids', which would spring up seemingly out of nowhere. During one, a crashing sound woke Christina. Her mother was inside her closet, in a rage, tearing clothes off the hangers and flinging them out into the room. Then she came and dragged Christina out of bed by her hair and took her to the closet. 'No wire hangers! No wire hangers!' she shouted, before pounding her daughter's ears until they rang. On another occasion, her mother – who was obsessed with cleanliness – woke Christina in the night ranting and raving that her dressing room floor, which her daughter had been ordered to clean that day as a punishment for some forgotten crime, had soap streaks on it. When Christina said she couldn't see them, that earned her a back-handed slap. Joan then grabbed a can of scouring powder and beat her daughter over the head with it until it burst open, exploding the white stuff all over the room – not to mention in Christina's hair and mouth. For several hours afterwards, through the night, Christina worked to clean it up, sobbing throughout.

At Christmas and birthdays Christina was given a vast number of presents from friends and her mother's fans but she would be allowed to keep only a very few inexpensive items that her mother picked out for her. The rest would be stored, to be re-wrapped and given to other children throughout the year. Yet every gift received had to be acknowledged with a hand-written thank-you note. Hours and hours would be spent trying to write charming letters for presents that would never be enjoyed. If there was a single mistake, the whole note had to be started again from scratch. Christina was never allowed to write her notes in pencil, only ink.

When Christina was ten years old, she was asked on a Friday if she liked the idea of boarding school. By Sunday, her mother had packed her up and driven her to one. Christina had no chance to say goodbye to her old teachers and friends. At the school, the teachers were told to monitor Christina as strictly as she had been at home. After any misdemeanours, Christina would be punished by being refused permission to leave the school grounds, sometimes even disallowed from going home for the holidays. Up to seven months went by at a time with Christina grounded at the school, unable to visit friends or even see her mother.

As an adult, Christina tried to have a relationship with her mother, always believing that Joan might really love her. For some time, they seemed to enjoy genuine companionship, going to glamorous functions together and with Christina visiting her often in her apartment, despite her mother's increasingly heavy drink problem. But when the curtains came down on Joan's life, Christina discovered that she had been disinherited – omitted from her mother's will. It was her mother's final slap round her face from the grave.

Film fans among you will have spotted that this case study comes from *Mommie Dearest*, the memoir written by Christina Crawford about her childhood with her famous mother, the 1940s Hollywood star, Joan Crawford. The book was made into a movie, which has become a cult hit, starring Faye Dunaway as the demonic filmstar. The film actually omits a lot of the abuse described in the book. The events were rubbished by Christina's two other siblings, although not by her brother, Christopher, all of whom were also adopted. Joan Crawford's OCD and apparent alcoholism do not necessarily mean that she was a psychopath. But there are, nevertheless, some interesting parallels to be drawn.

One type of psychopathic parent believes that the child is an extension of themselves – in other words, they do not recognise the boundaries between themselves and their child as an individual. (This is also symptomatic of a narcissistic parent.) This is why Joan would fly into a rage when her daughter displayed an 'imperfection' – such as having wire hangers in her closet. If the mother appears to bond with her child, it is not with the real personality but with a fantasy child. Hence, Joan's elaborate birthday parties for her daughter, which were amazing to look at but to which few – if any – of her real friends would be invited and after which all the presents would be taken away from her.

Lacking any empathy, a psychopathic parent will often manage their childcare mechanically. It can be as if their child is a doll; they are unable to attune to their baby's needs and so will neglect its crying or soiled nappy. The child may even be viewed as a mere commodity – in Joan and Christina's case at one point in the book she admits that the adoption of a blue-eyed, blonde-haired baby was a publicity stunt. Less glamorously, a psychopathic mother may use her children in order to claim more welfare benefits.

Shockingly, one modern parental habit of telling our children how brilliant they are could be construed as psychopathic. A psychopathic parent may pump up the child's own sense of grandiosity – telling the child they are as amazing as *they* believe themselves to be. These parents actively prevent the child from developing a realistic concept of him or herself. Think of the snotty teenage brat who is convinced that he is headed for a first class honours law degree despite failing every end-of-year exam.

Most parents, of course, simply want the very best for their child. But can you love a child *too* much? Might concern and protectiveness for your child breed, if not a psychopath, then at the very least a narcissist? Sometimes it can be difficult to see the difference between a parent's enormous love for a child and a parent who views the child as an extension of their own idealised self. Lisa is one such parent.

THE SEVEN SIGNS OF A PSYCHOPATHIC PARENT

When Lisa fell pregnant she embraced the idea of motherhood wholeheartedly. She bought long, flowery maternity dresses and she spent many happy hours in the park daydreaming about the beautiful son that would be born to her. Despite having hardly ever held a baby in her arms before, she was soon telling the other mothers in the antenatal class how they must bring up their children and even interrupting the teacher with her own advice.

Sign 1 Lisa's enthusiasm for her unborn child might seem loving but it's not about the baby – it's about her. She's showing grandiosity – an inflated view of her own abilities as a mother before motherhood has even begun.

Happily, her son, Jake, was born healthy and as he grew up Lisa enjoyed the comments of others on his well-chosen outfits and mop of golden curls.

Lisa was eager that her son would be the brightest and best of all children and from an early age he would be forced to sit alone in his room for hours doing 'homework' that she had set him. Once he started school, he was remarkably advanced for his years. When the teachers praised him in front of Lisa, she would scoop him up and kiss him, declare him her 'angel boy' and thank the staff for being so wonderful with him. Lucky Jake, thought the teachers, to have such a loving and charming mother.

Sign 2 Lisa's 'pride' in her son is in fact just an extension of her grandiosity – viewing Jake as an extension of an idealised version of herself. Furthermore, Lisa may know how to be a 'loving mother' in front of others – but at home it was a different story. Kisses and cuddles were notably absent because Lisa could display only shallow emotions. Any feeling shown was without depth, dramatic and short-lived.

Jake was a good little boy and a fast learner. But he'd been taught that he had to be. Lisa would laugh as she told friends that she'd get so cross when Jake got a spelling wrong or failed a test at school – but then, she'd say, he never makes the same mistake twice. So, really, her quick temper might be upsetting but it really got results. The other mothers would just stare at their feet.

Sign 3 Lisa's temper will have had a lasting and impressionable effect on such a small boy but she shows no remorse.

In his old-fashioned outfits – velvet coats and white knee-socks – Jake was frequently an object of ridicule at his school. Soon, he began to cry as he was left at the school gates. Lisa just ignored him. When his teachers called her in to suggest that maybe she could think about dressing him in a slightly more modern fashion, she said it was the bullies who should learn that some people are different. Why go after Jake, she questioned, you should be targeting the boys who are taunting him.

Sign 4 It's probably a fair point that Lisa makes here – that the bullies need to be changing their views, not Jake changing his clothes – but her ability to ignore her son's cries at the school gates displays a shocking callousness, an inability to attune to her child's emotional needs.

When Jake is eight years old it is discovered that he needs glasses. He had been having headaches after school for months. He only needs them for reading but Lisa sees an opportunity here. Times are tough and Jake's dad, from whom she separated when Jake was only a few weeks old, has been missing child maintenance payments. Lisa starts to claim disability benefits for her 'blind' son.

Sign 5 Lisa's reaction here is clearly that of a psychopath – she has spotted an opportunity to make money out of her child. She is a con artist.

As Jake gets older, he finds that Lisa's close interest in him doesn't extend to his physical wellbeing. While she still monitors his test results and pores over his school reports, quite often she will forget to cook him supper. She has a new job, as a PA to a CEO in the City, and she says she is too busy and tired to think about him all the time. He's eleven years old, she says, surely he can put a pizza in the oven?

Sign 6 Along with the absent, unreliable father, Lisa is showing signs of severe irresponsibility. She may be working hard to pay the mortgage but she has no sense of the urgent need to look after her young son.

Meanwhile, Jake is getting pushed more and more. At school his teachers are under strict instructions from Lisa to ensure that he spends one break time a day on extra maths. Twice a week, at lunchtime, he has piano lessons. After school, he is doing football twice a week and swimming twice a week. Weekends are spent going over his homework, handwriting exercises and watching 'improving' DVDs. He is allowed one hour of television a week. Jake doesn't have many friends but his mother has mapped out an illustrious future that includes Oxford University and qualifying as a surgeon by the time he is thirty. However, last year she thought he could be a lawyer and no doubt next year she'll be fixed on a career as an oil engineer. Unfortunately, by the time he is sixteen years old, Jake has yet to pass an exam with more than a C grade.

Yet he now believes in his mother's dream too.

Sign 7 Lisa is the ultimate 'helicopter parent' – hovering behind her child, never out of reach, whether he needs her there or not. But her relentless pushing of Jake despite his clear lack of academic ability reflects a lack of realistic long-term goals. Sadly, this attitude has had the worst effect of all – Jake has become a narcissist.

QUIZ: BRING UP BABY THE PSYCHOPATHIC WAY

I.   Your three-year-old wakes up at 3 a.m. She has done this every night for the last two weeks, crying until you go to her. You:

A) Explain gently that she is not allowed to do this and tuck her up in bed.

B) Ignore her. Why didn't that whisky in her milk bottle work?

C) Take her into bed with you. Your partner can sleep on the sofa.

2. Your baby's nappy needs changing. It's the seventh time today. You are tired from a night of little sleep, a gruesome trip to the supermarket with the baby crying and then one of the bags split on the way home. You:

    A) Sigh. Several times. Loudly. But you know there is nothing for it – you just have to grin and bear it. Then the baby smiles and you remember why it's all worth it.

    B) Only realise because the smell has got so bad. You change it hurriedly. Then put the baby back in the playpen and get back to your TV show.

    C) Embrace the opportunity to breathe in the natural smells of your beautiful baby. You would let her run around without a nappy, so that she could feel completely natural, but your partner complains about the stains on the rush matting.

3. It's parents evening at your child's school. You:

    A) Look forward to it. It's a good chance to catch up on what the teachers think about your child.

    B) Go with a list of prepared questions and an egg timer to make sure the other parents' don't go over their allotted time.

    C) Refuse to go. You are not going to engage in their overbearing patriarchal system.

4. Your thirteen-year-old son has been caught smoking at school. You:

    A) Give him a stern lecture about the dangers of smoking and take away his pocket money for a fortnight.

B) Laugh, give him a packet of Benson & Hedges and offer him a light.

C) Weep copiously for several hours about the certain premature death of your child. Then take him to the local cancer unit and leave him to sit for two hours next to someone dying of lung cancer.

5.   The mother of your daughter's best friend calls – she's caught her planning an illicit trip to a music festival. Your daughter was in on it. You:

A) Ask her why she felt the need to hide the fact that she was going to a music festival. You might have been able to work out a compromise.

B) Take the door of her bedroom off the hinges. There will be no secrets now.

C) Are deeply confused. You were hoping to go to the festival with your daughter. You had planned the picnic and the tent. Does she not want to hang out with her parents?

6.   It's sports day at your kids' school and you are entering the Parents' Race. You:

A) Limber up a little beforehand but know that in your jeans and plimsolls you have about as much chance of winning as an unaided potato.

B) Don your lycra shorts and spiked running shoes.

C) Refuse to participate. You and your kids are winners in life without awards or gold stars.

7.   You discover that your nineteen-year-old daughter has lost her virginity. You:

A) Take a cup of tea up to her room, tell her that if she wants to talk about it, you're here for her but understand she may want privacy.

B) Forbid her from leaving the house without your permission.

C) Arrange for all her friends to come over for a bonfire party to celebrate.

8. **Your son has stayed out all night, despite having promised to come home at 11pm. When you hear his key turn nervously in the lock at 8am, you:**

A) Hug him and then get immediately very cross – you were so worried. How could he not at least have called you? He is grounded for a fortnight.

B) Make him give up his mobile phone to you. You then drive over it several times, totally wrecking it, before handing it back. You do not speak to him for a week.

C) What's the problem? You were out with him. You just got back an hour earlier.

9. **Your son brings home his new girlfriend. He never brings girls home – this must be serious. You:**

A) Invite her to stay for supper with the family and only slightly embarrass your son by asking her lots of questions about herself.

B) Sit her down and inform her carefully that there will be no sex before marriage. You grill her on her family background, hobbies and food preferences and tell her you want to discuss this with her family too.

C) Send them straight up to bed and take them up a tray of breakfast the next morning.

10. **It's your daughter's wedding day. You:**

A) Weep a little in the morning – your little girl is finally gone. But it's a blissfully happy day for you and you thoroughly enjoy the party.

B) Refuse to attend. This is the ultimate betrayal. You stay home and get very drunk.

C) Have helped them organise it all in a field complete with a fete so that all the locals can join in too.

Answers:

Mostly A's: You're pretty normal and have a functioning, healthy, even loving relationship with your children.

Mostly B's: You are definitely a psychopath – overly controlling, self-interested and just plain nasty. If you don't bring up a psychopathic child, you will certainly raise someone fearful and desperate to escape you as soon as possible. I hope they succeed.

Mostly C's: You want to do everything for your child – but perhaps too much. You are not psychopathic but you really could back off a bit.

IS A PSYCHOPATH BORN OR MADE?

According to numerous studies and research, particularly those involving brain scans, there are strong indications that psychopathy is a genetic condition. At the very least, one might say that there is a genetic disposition that might lead a certain person in the right (or rather, wrong) environment to develop full-blown psychopathy.

So, could a parent knowingly breed a psychopath? There have been links, for example, between a problematic birth and maternal rejection to later criminal activity.[39] But while attachment difficulties might be associated with psychopathy they are unlikely to be the cause of it. It is equally likely that the psychopathic child causes emotional disturbance within the family.

However, the manner in which a psychopathic child is raised will have an influence on how those tendencies are carried through into later life. A violent upbringing will raise a violent psychopath. A well-educated, middle-class, motivated psychopathic child may become a very successful psychopathic adult, able to manipulate intelligently on a terrifying yet non-violent level. At least with the former, there's a better chance he will get caught and locked up.

THE MOTHER WHO KIDNAPPED HER OWN DAUGHTER

In February 2008, a nine-year-old girl, Shannon Matthews, was reported as missing by her mother, Karen. Coming hot on the heels of the Madeleine McCann story, the media was instantly fired into a campaign to help find the missing child, with one tabloid offering a £50,000 reward for information that led to Shannon's recovery.

In the Matthews' hometown of Dewsbury, Yorkshire, a massive search operation was fired up, involving over 300 police and members of the public. Eight hundred suspects were identified. An estimated £3.2million was spent on the police hunt until, twenty-four days later, Shannon was found.

Public relief was, however, short-lived. It was quickly revealed that Shannon had been discovered hidden in the base of a divan bed in a house belonging to her mother's boyfriend's uncle. The mother was soon found to have been involved in the 'kidnapping'.

The back story that subsequently unravelled makes it

149

difficult in some ways to see what was psychopathic in Karen's behaviour and what was the consequence of her low IQ (74), low self-esteem and low socio-economic background. She had seven children by four different fathers – with each of whom she had been involved for around two years, although the current boyfriend, who was ten years younger – and later was found guilty of possession of child pornography images on his computer – had been with her for four years. Domestic violence was a feature of several of her relationships.

Her parents spoke to the papers to say that she was unfit to be a mother, particularly since she had taken up with the latest boyfriend. Even her sister claimed that when Karen would drop off one of her children, at six months old: 'He would have a carrier bag or towel taped to his bum. Instead of spending money on nappies, she would spend it on stuff like crisps, sweets and pop.'

Karen was sentenced to eight years' imprisonment for kidnap, false imprisonment and perverting the course of justice. She has never pleaded guilty, claiming that her boyfriend told her to take the blame and that she was too frightened not to.

In an interview with a tabloid newspaper a year after she was jailed, Karen was asked what she missed about life on the outside. She said: 'Sex, shopping and coffee at my neighbours' house.' There was no mention of any of her seven children.

Much of what we know about Karen Matthews from newspaper and television reports chimes with features of psychopathic behaviour: her lack of care for the suffering of her child, the use of her child for financial gain, the constant lies and the false emotion displayed when pleading for her daughter's return.

PARENTS WHO CREATED A MEDIA STORM

On 15 October 2009, television viewers in America watched appalled as a runaway homemade helium balloon travelled fifty miles in the air apparently with a six-year-old boy alone inside. But just hours later, that boy, Falcon Heene, was discovered hiding in a cardboard box in his parents' attic.

Parents Richard and Mayumi Heene, who have twice appeared on ABC's *Wife Swap* reality TV show, are keen storm chasers. They had built the balloon as a meteorological device and it was thought that Falcon was concealed in a hidden compartment when it accidentally took off, reaching 7,000 feet in altitude at times. News channels covered the balloon's flight path in Fort Collins, Colorado, USA, military helicopters were engaged and Denver International Airport was briefly shut down. When the balloon finally came down in a field without the boy inside, people feared the he had fallen out and there was a frantic search on the ground below the flight path. But only hours later, Falcon was discovered, at home, safe and sound. He said he had been playing with his toys and had a nap.

But suspicions soon arose that the whole event had been a hoax – a clever ruse by the parents who were chasing a storm of a different kind, a media storm. In a television interview with CNN's *Larry King Live* after the event, Falcon said he had heard people calling his name (investigators had in fact searched the house twice but missed him). 'Why didn't you come out?' his father asked. 'You guys said that, um, we did this for the show,' his son replied. Asked what his son meant by this, the father bristled – he said he didn't know what his son meant. But nor did he ask his son to clarify.

Just three days later, the county sheriff stated that the parents would face felony charges. On 13 November 2009, Richard Heene pleaded guilty to the charge of attempting to influence a public servant. He was later sentenced to ninety days jail, and his wife to twenty days jail. They were also ordered to pay $36,000 in restitution and penalties.

BRIAN BLACKWELL'S PARENTS – NORMAL AND LOVING OR THE CREATORS OF A MONSTER?

In the last chapter, we looked at the case of Brian Blackwell, a young man who was charged for the manslaughter of his parents. Apparently successful – good at tennis and academically excellent – there appeared to be few reasons why Brian should have turned on his mum and dad in the way that he did.

Brian was diagnosed with Narcissistic Personality Disorder (a close cousin of psychopathy) and this was given as the cause of his actions. But is it possible that Brian's parents raised him to be this way?

Over the course of several interviews with Brian (which he agreed could be publicly disclosed), I learnt of some shocking details about his upbringing. Of course, we have to bear in mind that he will adapt his story to try to diminish his responsibility for the killings by putting the blame onto his parents, so we must treat his statements with caution.

Firstly, Brian's mother did all she could to keep him in a state of infantilism (perhaps causing arrested development at the psychopathic toddler stage). He claims that she insisted on bathing and dressing him right up until the night before he killed her – he was eighteen years old – even putting him in a bath of cold water if his behaviour was bad. He also says that she would not allow him to have his hair cut – she liked his naturally curly hair and would always cut it herself. When he was sixteen years old, his friends persuaded him to have his hair cut. He later told them that his parents went mad: they told him they were going to complain to the school and wouldn't let him eat at the kitchen table with them for a week.

His mother was also apparently excessively controlling with regards to his friends: as a young boy, he wasn't allowed any and was not allowed to play with the next-door neighbours, whom his mother considered 'gypsies' because they owned horses and had several children. As a teenager, he was very rarely allowed to go out and socialise; on the rare occasions when he could, he had to be back home by 9.30 p.m. Brian told someone with whom he played tennis that he had stayed out all night once and when he got home his mother told him, 'You have killed your father.' Apparently he had had a heart attack during that evening.

There is a hint at an overly close physical bond between mother and son. Brian claims that from twelve years old, he began sleeping in his mother's bed at night as his father was away and his mother 'liked the closeness'.

With regards to his school-life, his parents were minutely involved. At parents' evenings, his mother would take detailed notes, even producing Brian's previous reports for comparisons. Other parents were reportedly irritated by her taking up to forty minutes with each teacher instead of the ten minutes allocated. His parents picked his A-level subjects for him and, shortly before he was killed, Brian's father was calling UCAS and changing Brian's university choices.

His father was equally controlling in other ways – Brian claimed that his father would intimidate him with a handgun, firing it once so close to his ear that it caused him hearing difficulties (at ten years old, Brian was seen by the GP for possible hearing loss). His father would measure Brian every single day – on the day he killed his parents, Brian was 5 feet 10.75 inches tall. And it was noted that his father took his son's tennis very seriously – punishing him verbally when he didn't perform well enough – and was seen frowning, making faces and gesticulating from the side of the court.

Brian himself displays the core characteristics of a psychopath but it is apparent that his relationship with his parents was dysfunctional. If you look to the Blackwell case for an answer on the nature vs nurture question, it can't give you a black-

and-white solution, but it does demonstrate how devastating the consequences can be when biological and environmental factors interact.

IS PSYCHOPATHY A REPRODUCTIVE STRATEGY?

Evolutionary psychologists have proposed that psychopathy is a viable reproductive strategy. Harris and Rice have pointed out that many characteristics of the psychopath – sensation-seeking and a propensity for violence – would have been useful for impressing the opposite sex in caveman times and could therefore be Mother Nature's way of ensuring the next generation.[41]

Psychopaths are typically promiscuous and unfaithful; Hare has speculated that this is likely to result in both male and female psychopaths having lots and lots of children, although they are unlikely to care for them very well (if indeed they become involved in their lives at all).[42] As Hare puts it: 'The mobile, nomadic lifestyle of psychopaths . . . can be seen as part of a constant need for fresh breeding grounds.'[43]

The argument against this is that the risk-taking aspect of a psychopath doesn't fit the profile: it's not easy to pass on your genes if you are constantly risking your life with the dangerous pursuits many psychopaths often follow (drugs, fast driving and so on).

SUMMARY AND ADVICE

As the most influential figure in a young child's life, the psychopathic parent is uniquely placed to exert the most sinister intentions on a vulnerable and unquestioning victim.

One kind of psychopathic parent tends to see the child as an extension of their own selves, thereby putting them under pressure to behave within very strict parameters of expectation. The problems can really begin when the child starts to assert their own personality, challenging the parent and probably bringing horrific punishments on themselves.

Another kind of psychopathic parent sees the child as an opportunity for exploitation: using the child to claim benefits or even pretending their child is sick in order to gain wider sympathy and charitable donations.

Both kinds of psychopathic parent will be mechanical in the care of their children: there will be little or no physical affection (any embraces will usually be performed only publicly). A lack of a sense of responsibility means the children will have their basic needs unattended for long stretches of time.

Those who are brought up violently will – whether psychopathic or not – most likely go on to behave aggressively themselves. The influence of a criminal family will encourage a child to go the same way (see more in Chapter 6: Is Your Child A Psychopath?).

Of course, the young child of psychopathic parents is not in a position to help themselves. We can only hope that they have either extended family, teachers at school or Social Services watching out for them. But the grown child can. If you believe your parent is psychopathic, then protect yourself as far as you are able. Refuse to get drawn in by their emotional blackmail. Meet them outside either their or your home: it makes it easier to walk away when you feel that you have spent long enough with them. If you have siblings, talk to them about how you feel: perhaps they share the same reactions as you and together you can support each other.

Remember that someone who abuses you does not deserve to be a part of your life, even if they are your parents. Do not feel under any obligation to give them money or a room in your house. If you have created your own family now, make them the priority.

The good news is that a psychopathic parent is unlikely to

hang around. Many lose interest in their child early on – particularly when that child fails to conform to their expectations that he or she will be a mini-me carrying out their every wish. If, as an adult, you fail to be useful to them, you can expect them to move on pretty quickly. Just say goodbye and concentrate your love and happiness on those who deserve it.

8

IS YOUR PARTNER A PSYCHOPATH?

If your partner is a psychopath, it's highly possible that you don't know it. This may seem hard to believe – surely, you know best the person closest to you? But love can be blind. An unexplained bill here, a mystery phone call there – it's easy to explain them away.

More significantly, a psychopathic partner will have groomed you into staying with him despite repeated hurtful behaviour. A psychopathic partner will be good at appearing to be loving. Interspersing this with manipulation – in which they beat a partner into submission through a pattern of rewards, punishments and threats – the victim will be stripped of the necessary self-esteem and will to escape.

Once the psychopath has exhausted the usefulness of the partner, he will abandon them. For the victim, there will be relief but it will be short-lived. A psychopathic partner will return again and again, always promising change and never delivering it.

Tom turned my world upside down and I loved him for it. I was single, bored and frustrated in my job as a dental hygienist and although I was only twenty-seven years old, I felt as if I was just a year or two off giving up, buying myself a pair of sensible shoes and settling down into middle age on my own.

I noticed Tom right away. He had perfect teeth, straight and white, and quite quickly he requested me personally as his hygienist when he came in to get them cleaned once a month. He always took the time to ask me how I was and he was such a good listener that, over a few appointments, I ended up telling him all about how my parents had died in a car crash when I was nineteen years old; that I loved black and white movies, sushi and my cat Suze. In turn, he would impress me with his stories of what he'd been up to since the last time I'd seen him. It was clear he was a very successful businessman, although I never really understood exactly what it was that he did. Something in the City, I supposed. He made me laugh, too. Like when he told me about the time he ordered a thousand Ferrero Rocher chocolates to serve at a party where the British ambassador was guest of honour.

Before long, he was finding excuses to drop by even more frequently – whether it was to leave me a book he'd told me about or a trinket he'd brought me back from his latest business trip. I tried to pretend at first that I was too professional to submit to his advances but of course I was smitten. No one had ever flattered me like that before.

On our first date, he picked me up in his gleaming red Porsche – I later found out he'd sweet-talked the local dealership into lending it to him for a 'test drive' – and took me to dinner at a swanky restaurant. The kind that you have to book three months ahead if you're not a celebrity. To be honest, I felt about a heartbeat away from fainting the whole time I was there. But Tom was sweet – he had his arm around me and ordered my meal and wine for me. Over dinner he told me he'd never met anyone as lovely as me and he kept stroking my hair. It's my one asset, you see – my face is OK, I'm quite pretty when I'm happy – but I have long, silky blonde hair which is tightly held up in a bun when I'm at work. Tom had happened to see it when on one of his appointments in the surgery – I'd been retying it and thought I was out of sight of anyone. He says he was instantly captivated.

He took me home and kissed me at the front door. He said he knew he was coming on strong but he just felt so intensely. I didn't want to let him go but he said he'd call me and it wouldn't be long before he would hold me in his arms again.

In the end, he didn't call me for two weeks, by which time I was nearly frantic. He apologised so beautifully though, explaining that he'd been called away to an emergency business trip in New York and there just hadn't been time to call. I was so relieved to see him again I didn't press him with any questions.

Within a month, he'd moved in. Well, I say that but he didn't have many things – just some clothes, a few books and a rather extensive range of bathroom products. He explained he was so used to travelling and staying in hotels that he'd simply never acquired more stuff. Somehow it never crossed my mind to ask him where he was moving from.

When we got married, just six months later, it was the happiest day of my life. It was just the two of us. He said it was better that way – it was our private thing and, besides, my aunt had a habit of spoiling occasions. This was true: when she'd come over for supper to meet Tom she'd irritated him by asking too many questions instead of just relaxing and allowing herself to be charmed by him.

For the first few months, everything was perfect. He was away on business a lot but I was very understanding and he always brought me back a little present or two. Over time, there were some small things that did seem to be a bit odd. Like, he had two mobile phones but I only knew the number for one of them. He said he had to have an open line at all times in case an important business call came through. But he kept them close by him – always in his pocket or by his side of the bed.

He never offered any help with housekeeping money either. But I didn't feel I could really ask – it wasn't as if it cost that much more to have him there than when I was on my own. And I was reasonably comfortable for money, having inherited from my parents – I didn't have a mortgage, at any rate. Anyway, it was my choice that I always wanted to spoil him when he was home – it's not as if he ever asked for lobster suppers or caviar treats.

I never saw the Porsche again, of course. But he explained that it was more sensible for him to have an unostentatious car seeing as it spent most of its time parked at airports. So he would use mine. That was fine. I only had to take a couple of buses to work and the supermarket was a short walk away. I didn't really have many friends to go and visit. Besides, I was too caught up in Tom to have room for anyone else in my life.

I spent a lot of time cleaning the house. He liked it to be immaculate and would sulk for hours if he thought the bed hadn't been made properly or if he found dust on the mantelpiece. The only time he truly terrified me was when he found hair in the bath plug-hole and said if it happened again he'd throw Suze, my darling cat, out of the window. To show he meant business, he dangled her by the scruff of her neck as he said it. I didn't always know when he'd be home so I'd have to make sure the fridge was always full and there was something delicious for supper. He once came back and I only had beans on toast to offer. I kept telling him I was sorry but he was so angry – he threw the plate at the wall, stormed out and disappeared. I didn't hear from him for a fortnight. I didn't ever want to go through that again.

I know now it must sound crazy that I stayed with him. But I was so in love – he was my world. And when he was nice, he was . . . amazing. Loving and thoughtful.

The oddities did keep on coming though. He always had a ready and plausible explanation but I'd find myself tossing and turning in the night when he wasn't there, worrying. Cash would go missing from my purse and when I told him I couldn't find it, he'd say I was such an airhead I'd probably spent it without realising. Or he'd explain that someone had come to the door collecting money for charity and he hadn't liked to send them away without anything. Tom never had any post (he said it all went to his office) but I once found a credit card bill in his suit pocket that frightened me. It was for several thousand pounds and the address for him was a residential one – but not ours. He just said it was another business account.

One day, he came to me and said he'd had enough of the business he was in. He had a new idea, a brilliant scheme and it would *mean that he wouldn't have to go away so much and we could be together even more, maybe have children. He just needed a proper investment to start it up, around £250,000. When I asked if he could get a bank loan, he said no, they would interfere too much. It was such a forward-thinking idea they wouldn't have the insight to understand it. So why didn't we sell the house and use the profit? We could live somewhere smaller and it wouldn't be for long – this new business would make us rich.*

You'll think me a fool. But he was my husband – I wanted him to be happy and I was so excited at the idea of spending more time with him. I believed in him, too – he was obviously such a success at work, in ways that I could never understand. If anything, I felt grateful to be given the chance to help him – I felt as if he needed me for the first time, and that felt wonderful.

Of course, I gave him the cheque and just a week or so after it cleared, he went on another business trip and never came back. For a couple of weeks, I tried not to worry – he might have just been called away. But then I got scared: his phone wouldn't pick up. I realised then that we had no friends in common; I didn't even know a single member of his family that I could call. Eventually, I reported him missing to the police and they came back to me a few weeks later: his name was an alias. His real name was Paul, he was wanted for credit card fraud and, now they knew about me, bigamy. He had another wife, just twenty-five miles away, and a boy of seven.

Tom, or Paul I suppose I should say, is in prison now. He writes to me occasionally, saying he is lonely – he says he gave me all those happy times and now he has nothing, that I should take pity on him. Sometimes, I think I might write back.

Jennifer, 36, ex-wife

Are you living with a psychopathic partner? It might be hard to tell. It would be nice to think that you'd know. But he won't be wearing a bell round his neck that sounds a helpful ring of alarm. (We're dealing here with mental rather than physical abuse – regardless of your partner's psychological make-up you must seek help if you are a victim of domestic violence.) Reading Jennifer's story, you may think you have spotted plenty of clues – which we'll look at shortly – and perhaps you think she was an idiot for staying with him. But love is blind, isn't it? How many of us have forgiven a missed phone call, an unexplained bill, a story that didn't quite add up? Jennifer saw that some pieces of the puzzle didn't quite fit but she was crazy for him and, as she says, most of the time he was loving and thoughtful.

The confusing thing is that psychopaths can trick their victims with a well-honed *appearance* of loving behaviour. If they're clever, they'll have learned the right social behaviours to fool most of the people, most of the time. When a psychopath wants to divert your attention from a telling indication of his true nature, he'll tell you he loves you. Of course, he doesn't *feel* that.

Let's look at the Jennifer and Tom story more closely and see what she could have picked up on if she had known to be more alert.

We know that Tom *is* a psychopath, and as such has demonstrated the often seen 'assessment–manipulation–abandonment' process on his victim. 'A–M–A' is a psychological model observed to underpin psychopaths' relationships; it has been studied between psychopaths and their work colleagues but operates just as effectively in their more intimate lives.

First of all, Tom assessed Jennifer to see whether she would make a good – that is, susceptible and compliant – partner. For some psychos, this can be an almost unconscious 'weighing up', for others, it is much more overt. I had one client who would hang around outside support groups, in order to have the best statistical chance of finding vulnerable women. Tom didn't go to quite these lengths and, luckily for him, it didn't take him long to find a girl with 'potential'; Jennifer readily admitted she was lonely, had little family to look out for her, was bored in her job and had financial means. Vulnerable and loaded: perfect.

Next, Tom had to groom Jennifer to prepare her for his own special brand of relationship. Grooming involves moulding a submissive partner via a baffling combination of tender moments, threats and penalties if they fail to behave as the psychopath wants. The first stage usually involves a full-on romantic assault – the Porsche, the romantic dinner, the declarations of intense feelings.

Psychopaths frequently imitate a Mills & Boon style of romance – chocolates, flowers, poetry. I had a client who used to go into card shops and learn the soppy sayings on the romantic cards to use on his girlfriend. You might be taken aback to start with but it can also be hard to resist, particularly for a person unused to such attention.

Here's something one client told me, which gives a pretty good insight into the way their mind works: 'I would call her a regular associate, not a girlfriend. The word girlfriend implies feelings for her that I have never had. I like her – but what is love? I like the fact that she provides me with convenient sex, she does things for me and gives me company. Is that love? I don't feel any more for her than I do for my dog.'

Or what about this, from another: 'I buy her flowers and tell her that I love her with all my heart. I don't really know what that means but I know that it puts a smile on her face and buys me what I want from her. Flowers are cheaper than paying my own rent.'

The second stage in the grooming process is often brief sulking and threats of rejection or abandonment if the partner fails to appreciate them. Jennifer learnt this when she didn't clean the house thoroughly enough or provide Tom with a good enough supper.

Following this is an introduction of minor bad behaviour, where the psychopath pushes the boundaries to see what they can get away with. We see this with Jennifer and Tom when he would go away without calling or take cash from her purse. And just as Tom told Jennifer that she was an 'airhead', so the psychopath will make a partner feel that they are being unreasonable and making a fuss about nothing if they complain. They will make them feel inferior. In every row, the victim will somehow find that they are the one apologising.

Then there is a steady escalation in unreasonable behaviour, punctuated by brief returns to the romantic onslaught. Jennifer is thrown into confusion because of Tom's 'mostly loving and romantic' presentation. It is this pattern of training that makes the victim putty in the psychopath's hands.

In the worst cases, a psychopath may manipulate a partner by responding to their reasonable complaints with unkind behaviour towards someone or something that means a lot to them – classically pets or children. Tom did this when he dangled Jennifer's beloved cat out of the window after she had failed to clean the bath properly. He also ensured that he isolated Jennifer from any sources of support or anyone who may start to challenge him by refusing her wish to invite her aunt or any friends to their wedding. Over time she was virtually cut off from everyone – her whole life revolved around Tom.

Finally, when Tom had exhausted everything he could get from Jennifer – somewhere to stay, her car, convenient sex, being fed and finally a quarter of a million pounds of her money – he abandoned her.

But even though he has been found out and imprisoned, he keeps returning – writing to Jennifer and asking to be taken back. This is something I often encounter in clinical practice, as psychopaths fail to appreciate the impact that they have had on other people's lives and feel entitled to reconciliation on demand. The most dangerous and damaging aspect of a psycho-pathic partner is that they will eventually attempt to come back, just like a bad smell in your blocked drain.

THE SEVEN SIGNS OF A PSYCHOPATHIC PARTNER

Looking at the A–M–A model is a good assessment of whether someone is involved with a psychopathic partner – but it is not conclusive. Let's take a look at how the psychopath's core characteristics frequently manifest within their relationships.

Mike is a twenty-seven-year-old championship league foot-baller in the Midlands. He's been married to Dawn for eight years – his management told him he should get hitched as soon as possible – and they have two small boys. He's got the Rolex, two flash cars in the driveway and a shih tzu lapdog for the missus. Dawn looks good, and she takes care to stay that way, but she's no fool: she knows her husband is a target.

Mike knows it too and is glad of it. He's had a couple of premier league football clubs sniffing around him and he's doing his best to deliver on the promise he showed when he first turned pro. But mostly he can't believe his luck – he's never happier than when he's got the opportunity to brag about his salary, his cars, the fact that he can give his kids the chances he never had.

One night he's in Bottoms Up, a lap-dancing wine bar in Cheshire, celebrating the goal he scored against Bolton FC. He's getting special attention from a dancer called Crystal. Like all the rest, Crystal is a proud faker: miles of bright white teeth, a tan verging on the citrus, prominently pert boobs and a stable's worth of extensions on her head. Mike is used to extra attention but something about Crystal seems different – for one thing, she listens to him.

It's not long before Mike is returning to Bottoms Up two or three times a week, and each time he puts in a request for

Crystal. Mike knows he is probably being very stupid indeed but she gives him so much pleasure and he is entranced by the fact that he cannot seem to hold onto her for long. Despite the interest she's shown in him, she teases him by making him watch while she dances for other customers.

Sign 1 Crystal genuinely needs to work and, in contrast with most of her fellow dancers, she finds her job both financially and personally rewarding. Like most psychopaths, her attitude to sexual behaviour is impersonal and she is keen to exploit its power over others. Pornography, prostitution, or more commonly pimping out others is rife between psychopaths. Crystal does not go this far, but she is prepared to nonchalantly use displays of her sexuality to manipulate and excite jealousy in Mike.

It's only a few weeks until Crystal has Mike right where she wants him – pinned beneath her manicured thumb. With much chin wobbling she told him that her landlord was threatening to evict her unless she could come up with the rent – so he paid it (three months back payment and three months up front). Mike is also hoping to encourage Crystal to work less by giving her generous wads of cash when he sees her. And whenever they walk past a jewellery shop or designer label boutique there always seems to be something in the window that Crystal has her eye on and Mike buys it. He enjoys Crystal's displays of gratitude when they are in bed later.

Sign 2 Classic psychopath behaviour here in that Crystal is leeching off Mike at every available opportunity. Admittedly, at this stage, it's difficult to see much difference here between Crystal and your everyday gold digger. Interestingly, psychopaths don't always pick off the weak and vulnerable – they also enjoy partners with status so they can benefit by association.

But Crystal's manners soon leave her. Mike is shocked when he witnesses her first change in behaviour: he forgot to open her side of the car first and was suddenly cowering beneath a barrage of expletive-laden abuse. After that, the irrational behaviour comes thick and fast and Crystal starts calling his house at all hours, screaming down the phone at him if he answers, hanging up if Dawn does. (Dawn is no fool – she knows what's going on but is too scared of losing her mini-mansion to confront him about it.) Last week, when Crystal discovered that Mike had taken Dawn out to dinner at a fancy restaurant (she found the receipt when she was going through his wallet) she drove round to his house at 3 a.m. and smashed all the flowerpots in his front garden. Then she smashed his car headlights.

Sign 3 Crystal has poor behavioural controls. Although she is exercising her cunning in manipulating Mike, her tendency for disproportionate anger and frustration if things are not exactly as she wants them to be, betray her psychopathic character.

No matter what Mike does for her, it's never enough. Mike has fallen for Crystal hook, line and sinker and is blind to her manipulations. But she is cold to his every move. Crystal never wants to cuddle after sex, she turns her head so his lips hit her cheek whenever he leans in and teases him for being 'pathetic' in bed. She even used her mobile phone to film him when he was having sex with her and threatens to show it to his wife. (He also thinks he walked in on Crystal showing her friend the footage; the pair were laughing hysterically.) Despite all this, Crystal tells Mike that she wants to take the relationship forward and move in with him; she talks endlessly about his filing for a divorce from Dawn so that they can have the big white wedding that she has always wanted.

Sign 4 Crystal's desire to marry Mike is surprising, particularly given the coolly abusive way she treats him. Commitment is not a concept that psychopaths compute – but they do understand the financial and other benefits that living with a partner can bring them. By the age of thirty, an archetypal psychopath will have thrown themselves into three or more ill-fated marriages/live-in relationships.

Finally, Mike snaps: he's had enough. He tells Crystal he wants to cool it. He deletes her number from his phone and books him and Dawn into a five-star country house hotel for a mini-break.

But he doesn't reckon on Crystal. She phones him every fifteen minutes for twenty-four hours. Then, when he still fails to respond, she leaves a beautifully wrapped box on his doorstep. It contains a dog turd. Finally, she texts him over and over again telling him she can't live without him.

So Mike caves in. On what was supposed to be a romantic weekend away together, Mike tells Dawn that he is leaving her. He calls Crystal when he gets back to the city and tells her he is a free man now, all hers. 'That's amazing news,' says Crystal. 'Hang on a sec, I've got to go – call you back later.'

She then disappears for two weeks. When she turns up again and Mike hysterically asks where she has been, she simply says: 'Away.' Crystal tells Mike he is making a fuss over nothing. 'Can we go out for supper now?' she asks. Case closed.

Sign 5 This chaos – hysterics, unexplained disappearances, ultimatums – are classic signals in a psychopathic relationship generating a series of rewards and punishments designed to draw the victim ever further in. They are also, of course, exactly what makes the relationship addictive.

Having now left Dawn, Mike is anxious to make his relationship with Crystal right. He suggests that they meet her family – he'd like to take her parents out for lunch. But he notices that she is always vague about her relations – he's not sure he has ever heard her say exactly where they live. Whenever Mike asks her about her past, she just seems to fudge the answer by claiming 'it's not very interesting' or telling him to mind his own business. If he thinks about it, Mike realises that Crystal changes her best friend on a weekly basis – she's always falling out with the other girls at the club – and when he suggested that they throw a party for her birthday, she quickly changed the subject. He wonders if she *has* any friends.

Sign 6 Mike should be alert to Crystal's fuzzy statements when it comes to her friends and family. As someone's 'significant other' you should expect knowledge of, and at least some degree of involvement in their world. Psychopath's relationships with family and friends tend to be stressed or inexplicably non-existent. If you don't get an invitation for tea with mother/auntie/best mate at some point, it may be that a psychopathic partner has changed their story so much that they can't be bothered to keep it up or they've cut off their relatives altogether.

What Mike doesn't know is that Crystal has three other men like him tagging along behind her. They're all paying for her rent, clothes and jewellery.

Luckily for Mike, he gets a last-minute escape from his entanglements with Crystal. Not that he was expecting it: as far as he knew, they were about to move in together. But one night Crystal met a premiership footballer at her club and decided that he was a better target than Mike and all the others put together. Mike didn't know it but he was left stranded in his new empty flat, the one he'd bought for them both to move into and for which he'd only picked up the keys that day. And the joint bank account she'd insisted they open, as a symbol of their being together? Emptied.

Sign 7 As if the manipulation, the conning, the lies, the shallow emotions, the parasitic behaviour and the sexual impropriety weren't enough, Mike learns that Crystal can walk away without even a sentimental backward glance. She may have had a cushy life with Mike, but abandoning him at the slightest sign of a better scam is just something Crystal can't help herself doing. Still, even though she may have scarpered now, Mike should watch out. It's more than likely that she'll come back just as he is getting his life back together.

ARE YOU ATTRACTIVE TO A PSYCHOPATH?

Consider these three different situations – can you recognise yourself in any of them?

Type A

One night, your boyfriend comes home at 4 a.m. and you spot a love-bite on his neck. You know he was out on a boys' night out and it obviously just got a bit out of hand: you know how women can prey on drunk men. You get up and make him an omelette and leave him to sleep off his hangover.

After having made plans, your partner suddenly tells you that he can't come to your sister's wedding next month – it clashes with the final of a snooker tournament he's been playing in and he's sure he's going to win. You understand and make his excuses to your family on his behalf.

At least you have the mini-break to look forward to. But the day before you are due to leave, he calls to say something has come up at work and he can't get away after all.

It's the third time this has happened and it's not as if he's a high-flier – he's an estate agent. You put the phone down and have a good cry, then get supper ready. It's not his fault and at least now you can get some odd jobs done around the house.

A few weeks later, you lend your car to your partner for him to take on a fishing trip with friends but when he comes back it is not only empty of petrol but filthy with beer cans and stinking bait. Not to mention the new dent in the rear end. Yet there are no apologies or explanations forthcoming. You think he must be waiting to say sorry with a grand gesture and rather than spoil it, you cook the fish for supper and send the car to the garage.

For your partner's birthday you have saved all year to buy him something you know he really wants – a motorbike. You've even ordered him a cake from the local patisserie. If you could, you'd throw him a surprise party but you don't know any of his friends very well and he doesn't like yours.

Your partner has gone on a business trip for a week and fails to get in touch at all except to tell you that he's on his way back from the airport. He's obviously been very busy and must be exhausted – you make sure there's a hot bath and supper waiting for him.

The following week, you have to go away yourself to see your parents. You ask your boyfriend to feed your cat. But when you get back, you find it mewling in the shed where it's been left with just the one bowl of cat food, long since eaten. He explains that he's developed a sudden allergy to your pet. You are sad but decide you had better find your beloved puss a new home.

Shortly after you receive a generous inheritance from your late aunt, your partner says he needs a loan of £10,000 (practically the whole amount). You say that you'd rather give it to him than lend it – it saves complications and anyway, what's yours is his.

One night, just as you're about to leave the house to go to a party your boyfriend tells you he doesn't like the dress you're wearing – it's too revealing. You sigh, but you know it's not worth the row and so take it off and change back into your usual jumper and jeans.

Type B

If your boyfriend should come home at 4 a.m. with a love-bite on his neck there's no way he's getting into bed with you. You leave him on the sofa – he's got some serious talking to do in the morning.

When he says he can't come to your sister's wedding, you tell him you understand. You understand that his priorities lie elsewhere and obviously not with you. You say that you are seriously considering breaking up with him over this.

When your mini-break is cancelled again at the last minute, you decide that you will go – just with your best friend instead.

When you see the state of your car after the fishing trip, you send your boyfriend straight back out with a bucket and sponge. You tell him that he'll be paying the garage bill and then you take him off the car insurance.

For his birthday, you bake him a chocolate cake. At this point, you're not feeling particularly generous towards him.

After his non-communicative business trip, your boyfriend returns home to find that you have gone out.

When you discover your neglected cat, you suggest that your partner goes to see the doctor to get his allergy checked . . . and that he doesn't bother coming back for a few days.

When your boyfriend asks to borrow the ten thousand pounds, you say that you need to know what it is for and that if you do lend it to him it will need to be repaid in instalments, with interest. He will have to sign a contract agreeing to this.

When your boyfriend tells you he doesn't like the dress you're wearing you say you won't take it off because you love it but you do compromise by wearing a jacket with it.

Type C

Your boyfriend stumbles through the bedroom door and shows you his love-bite. You slap his face and then the two of you have wild, make-up sex.

When your partner mentions the tournament and says it clashes with the wedding, you break his snooker cue in half.

At the news that the mini-break is cancelled, you decide that if Mohammed won't go to the mountain . . . and turn up at his office the next day with a Champagne picnic.

When your boyfriend gets back from the fishing trip you sweetly ask him to come in for a cup of tea. Then you stuff a fish in the exhaust pipe and tell him to drive the car home.

For his birthday, you surprise him at work with a kissogram – unfortunately, it arrives just as he is in a meeting with his boss.

If your boyfriend should ever dare to not keep in touch with you for as long as a week, he'll find the locks changed when he gets home.

After the starving-cat debacle, you 'forget' to feed your partner's goldfish when he next goes away and he comes back to find it floating on the top of the tank.

When your boyfriend asks to borrow the money you have inherited you say sorry you can't – you've already spent it on wise investments (a paid-off credit card bill, a designer handbag and a weekend in Paris).

When your partner tells you to take off the dress you're wearing you agree only if it means you can both skip the party and have an early night instead . . .

How did you do?

If you mostly fit the profile of Type A, you are a psychopath's dream, allowing him to control you in order to get what he wants (the key point here is that you don't know his friends and he doesn't like yours). He is not going to change but you can. Learn to love yourself and find a man who shows you respect.

If you mostly fit the profile of Type B, you are unlikely to get caught by a psychopath and if you are he won't hang around for long. He can't manipulate someone like you as long as you are on your guard.

If you recognise yourself in Type C, then you're certainly assertive. In fact, maybe just a little too much so. You're not in any danger of having a psychopathic boyfriend but perhaps you need to remember that compromise in a relationship is not a sign of weakness but of fairness.

HOW A PARTNER BECOMES A VICTIM

Following an episode of unacceptable behaviour, it is common for the psychopath to express regret (which is superficial). They may make promises to change their behaviour or go on a charm offensive, romancing their victim. At this stage – that is, immediately following the regrettable incident – the victim may be clear that the behaviour is unacceptable but, as the initial traumatic effects lessen over time, they are seduced by the assurances of the partner and return to, or remain in, the relationship. There often follows a period of calm and even romance, which is highly rewarding and reinforces the victim's optimism regarding the future. Maybe it was a one-off?

However, when tensions start to re-occur in the relationship, the victim readily recognises these and typically tries to change *their* behaviour in order to avoid further abuse (rather than chuck their partner out or warn them that this behaviour will not be tolerated). As the victim attempts to placate their partner, they may become more and more aware of the futility of doing so. This can lead to an escalation of fear, tension and emotional distress. Not that the psychopathic partner would necessarily notice: studies have shown that they find it difficult to distinguish fear and sadness in voice patterns.

In studies, children and adults who had displayed psychopathic tendencies were asked to listen to voice clips and describe the emotion therein but they had difficulty doing so.[44] A similar result was seen in a study where psychopaths were asked to name the emotional expression on the faces of others and it was shown that they were insensitive to fear, disgust and sadness.[45] They also found that when psychopaths and non-psychopaths were shown a face with a neutral expression that slowly changed to fear the psychopaths took significantly longer to identify the expression. A 75 per cent level of expression was necessary for them to spot the fear, compared to 65 per cent for non-psychopaths.

As a victim repeatedly finds that they are unable to protect themselves from whatever is going on and/or is subject to intermittent psychological abuse such as insults, put-downs and comments such as 'you made me do it', they come to perceive themselves as increasingly helpless and less powerful than their partner. Therefore, they frequently feel that they 'need' the other person in order to compensate for their own failings. This makes it extremely difficult for a victim to leave the relationship without strong external support.[46]

WHY DO WOMEN LOVE MEN ON DEATH ROW?

A curious thing I have noticed with my most dangerous incarcerated male clients is that they receive a lot of letters and attention from women previously unknown to them; anecdotal evidence indicates that the same happens with men on Death Row. It may also be a largely female thing – I haven't noticed that my most dangerous incarcerated women clients receive a similar number of letters and attention from men previously unknown to them. Why does this happen?

People who have intimacy problems may unconsciously choose partners who are physically or emotionally unavailable. This allows them to experience the heady rush of 'love' without having to deal with the – often mundane or difficult – reality of a relationship, or risk any true closeness.

A relationship with a Death Row prisoner is the ultimate expression of this. It can be intense and dramatic but it is 90 per cent fantasy. Let's face it, there is very little if any chance of this boyfriend turning up on your doorstep with his bags packed and ready to move his CD collection in. It enables the relationship to stay 'stuck' in the love-letters and telephone conversations stage, which normally characterises only the very initial stages of a relationship. This is both non-threatening and exciting.

I'm aware of some women who have found out that their prison 'boyfriend' has several women on the go, but have been prepared to ignore it as the arrangement perfectly meets their needs for a close-but-not-that-close fantasy relationship.

Furthermore, many women are attracted to the idea of reforming a bad boy with their love. These women may find the idea of man who is gentle and romantic with them but who has clearly been capable of extreme violence in the past, erotic and personally flattering. They tend to buy into their partner's excuses, justifications and rationalisations of their crimes so that they can be with them without feeling too much conflict.

In many ways these types of relationships are psychologically similar to those of women who develop 'crushes' on celebrities or other unavailable men. This has been linked with past loss (often of a child), and the women not wanting to risk the pain of loss in the future by having a 'real' relationship.

THE WIVES WHO 'KNEW NOTHING' – ROSEMARIE FRITZL AND PRIMROSE SHIPMAN

If you think that there's no chance you could be fooled by the sort of psychopathic partner that I've outlined above, consider those women who lived in total ignorance that their husbands were severely psychopathic. Two that spring to mind are Mrs Shipman and Frau Fritzl.

Rosemarie Fritzl married the now-notorious Josef Fritzl when she was seventeen and he was twenty-one. In 2008, aged seventy-three, he was sentenced to life imprisonment for fathering seven children with his daughter, whom he kept in the cellar beneath the family home for twenty-four years. One baby lived only three days and was 'cremated' in the wood incinerator; three lived as the 'downstairs family' with the daughter, Elisabeth; three lived upstairs with Rosemarie, adopted by her after Josef claimed their daughter had left them on the doorstep for them to raise, having run away with a cult.

Many have questioned how Rosemarie Fritzl could possibly have either ignored or not noticed the wheelbarrows of food that were taken down to the cellar and the fact that she was never allowed down there. Nor did she seem to be suspicious that her daughter would leave not one but three children on their doorstep. Many ask why she didn't do more to track down her daughter after her sudden disappearance.

But Josef Frtizl was a despot in the family home. Despite the fact that ten years into their marriage her husband was imprisoned for eighteen months on a charge of rape, she took him back. She also turned a blind eye to her daughter being repeatedly raped by her husband between the ages of eleven and eighteen before she 'disappeared'. It may have been fear that prevented her from asking too many questions of her husband and which finally led to 'extreme cognitive dissonance', a psychological condition in which two uncomfortable, conflicting feelings are reduced by an irrational logic. In Rosemarie's case, she will have made excuses for his behaviour, no matter how far-fetched they were.

Rosemarie, now estranged from her children and grand-children, has changed her name and lives alone in a small apartment in Austria. She is not exceptional – at least, only as exceptional as the occurrence of extreme psychopathic behaviour.

Primrose Shipman was married to Dr Harold Shipman, the GP who was sentenced to life imprisonment for the murder of fifteen of his patients by lethal injection and the forging of a will. It has been estimated that he was responsible for as many as 250 deaths. Primrose attended his trial, reportedly always the first to arrive and the last to leave, even handing out chocolates. A loyal wife of thirty-five years, she has only ever said that she remained 'convinced' of his innocence. This, despite the fact that she had long had to put her husband before everything else.

They met when she was seventeen and, after she fell pregnant a few months later, had a shotgun wedding in 1966, of which her strict Methodist parents heavily disapproved. In 1975, Dr Shipman was fined £600 and sent to drug rehabilitation for forging prescriptions of pethidine for his own personal use. His wife would drive him to and from home visits and explain away blackouts induced by his drug use as 'epileptic fits'. At work – and at home – he was reputed to be a bully, with irrational mood swings and a childish temper.

Yet, he wrote her romantic poetry from prison, she continued to visit him until his suicide four years after his sentencing and, according to newspaper reports, she still wears his wedding ring. Shipman was obviously capable of inspiring huge loyalty in his wife and able to create a depth of emotion and care in others that, given the cold and calculated nature of his crimes, he was unlikely to have experienced himself.

Occasionally a psychopath meets their chillingly 'perfect' match: 'I was waiting at Cheltenham bus station. He approached me and started talking. My first impression was, as I say, disgust! He was dirty, he seemed shifty and I didn't like the way he spoke. Of course, Fred could charm the birds out of the trees and after a fair bit of persuasion, I agreed to have a drink with him' Rosemary West said.

THE KILLER GIRLFRIEND – TRACIE ANDREWS

In December 1996, Lee Harvey, twenty-five, bled to death in a country lane. His fiancée, Tracie Andrews, claimed that a 'porky man with big staring eyes', had murdered him in an extreme road rage attack. This sparked a nation-wide manhunt and police interviewed 650 motorists but failed to find any suspects.

Following the attack, Andrews made emotional appeals on

television for the capture of the killer. She described her fiancé as a 'lovely, funny, caring' man and good father to his two daughters, both five years old, one from a previous relationship.

In fact, it was Andrews, then twenty-seven, who had cut his throat and stabbed him numerous times with a Swiss Army-type penknife. During the twenty-one-day trial, it emerged that the couple had had a volatile relationship. Their neighbour heard two-hour rows up to three times a week that were so loud she could make out what they were arguing about. They had had such an argument on the day of the murder.

Tracie's quick temper and signs of volatility here (she also attacked her boyfriend in public on a number of occasions) indicates poor behavioural controls. But the very shocking and potentially psychopathic element about Tracie's story is that she was able to go on television to beg for helping in finding her boyfriend's killer. Her protestations of innocence continued for some time and yet she neither showed remorse nor took responsibility – further red flags.

She was sentenced to life imprisonment, with the recommendation that she remain incarcerated for fourteen years. Andrews protested her innocence at the time of sentencing, admitting her guilt only in 1999 in an attempt to reduce her sentence. She is due for release in July 2011.

SUMMARY AND ADVICE

As in any other area of manipulation or fraud, a psychopath on the hunt for a partner will choose his victim carefully. He will either choose someone lonely and vulnerable, or a high achiever who gives him the status he desires. As a highly skilled manipulator he will use a series of rewards and threats to get his victim right where he wants them. Finally, when he has got what he wants, he will abandon them, leaving them bewildered and confused. Often, he will return again and again.

A relationship with a psychopath can be devastating indeed. But I understand that the dynamics of such a relationships can be powerfully addictive ('she loves me . . . she loves me not . . . she loves me . . .').

So how can you gain some perspective and maintain your self respect?

- The rewards of the good moments are strong. You need to ask yourself if you are dealing with love or an addiction. A good way to tell is to write down a list of your own personal values and boundaries in a relationship: do you value loyalty? Honesty? What is acceptable and what is not? Does your current relationship violate your values? If you are constantly compromising your beliefs about how a partnership should function, the chances are that your relationship has become a bad habit rather than a choice.

- Do a relationship audit: what percentage of the time do you feel content, happy, cared for? What percentage of the time do you feel used, dominated, anxious? Depending on the answers to these questions, it might be time to cut your losses and run. I admit this is easier said than done but at least get legal advice if necessary and surround yourself with professional and personal support.

- If you believe you are in a relationship with a psychopath you need first and foremost to recognise that they are not going to change their behaviour. In fact, you may find that it is you who needs to change in order to bring things back to your ideal. Unfortunately, no amount of love or forgiveness will engender the change that is needed. A psychopath is resistant to all forms of emotional appeal. Their behaviour may become a little more bearable with age but they cannot be 'cured'.

- If you cannot leave straightaway then protect yourself. On a practical level, for example, have you got a separate bank account? Make sure you keep an eye on any joint finances. Do what you can to assert yourself: refuse to give in to his whims and stop lending him money or being available for sex whenever he wants it.

- Do not enter into game-playing or power struggles: the situation will invariably escalate and you will only lose. Don't keep secrets from your friends or make excuses for your partner's behaviour towards them either. It's under-standable that you will feel embarrassed but this in itself is a clear sign that there is something wrong in the relation-ship. Your friends may not respond in the way that you want them to, but they will help you keep a proper perspective.

- Recognise that when you are being put down, shouted at or taken advantage of, you are being abused. See it for what it is and also bear in mind at all times that it is *not your fault*. Your partner may come up with a list of reasons why it is but inevitably they aren't real.

- Resist colluding with your partner's distorted version of events, particularly when they shift blame and responsi-bility for their unreasonable behaviour on to you. At the end of every row with a psychopathic partner it is always you who apologises. Practise using the phrase, 'Here's how I see it . . .' When they tell you that you are blowing things out of proportion, nod sagely and say, 'Well, that is what *you* believe.'

- Practise being assertive: speak in a calm, low tone in an 'I mean business' firm voice. Hold your head up, repeat what you need to say then simply disengage – leave the room, take the dog out for a walk, go shopping – just don't continue flogging a dead horse. The more you go over it and go around in circles, the more disorientated you become and the more likely you are to believe their spin. The chances are that if you are not a pushover your psychopathic partner will do you the inadvertent kindness of leaving you instead.

9

IS YOUR CELEBRITY CRUSH A PSYCHOPATH?

The charmer in ruthless pursuit of riches and fame ticks many of the psychopathic boxes. The problem for us is how to tell the difference between a superstar and a psychopath? Both can be charming, obsessively self-interested, frankly crackers when it comes to their personal demands and surrounded by an entourage that has been manipulated into serving their inflated sense of self.

A psychopathic celebrity is not, at first glance, a danger – they are, after all, at a safe distance. But it is my belief that the menace lies in their manipulation of you as their fan. If you look to a celebrity as your role model ('what would Elvis do?') then you may be encouraged to replicate psychopathic characteristics, which will not make you very popular with your friends and family. Unfortunately, in a society that reveres celebrity we are seeing this kind of behaviour on the increase as ordinary people clamour to be on reality TV shows and claim their 'right' to fame despite having no talent at all. Even those who are not on tele-vision may view narcissism and histrionic emotions as normal behaviour. This will not make for a pleasant world for us to live in.

I started working for Chrissie a year ago. I'm her twenty-ninth personal assistant in thirteen years. I've lasted the longest so far, probably because I've been around the block a few times. Her manager hired me against her wishes because I'm one of the few who won't stand for nonsense. But I have to admit – Chrissie has pushed me to my absolute limit at times.

As you know, Chrissie is a major movie star. She's won one Oscar, been nominated for three others and is a darling of the press. She's managed to cultivate this image of being a really down-to-earth, natural person who does lots of charity work and is a loving mother to her two children. Interviewers and fans who meet her are always charmed by her good manners and protestations that she loves nothing more than a plate of chips and half a Guinness in her local pub. But anyone who works for her knows a different story.

For a start, she's going through her third divorce right now and her two children have different fathers. They're finding all the change very upsetting but Chrissie doesn't seem to care about that. In fact, she rarely has just one man in her life – married or not, there are usually two or three being juggled at any one time and the children are expected to just roll with it. She's even told them to call any man they meet at breakfast 'uncle'. But regardless of whether they're feeling confused, Chrissie doesn't worry so long as they look good for the cameras when she does an 'at home' photoshoot and she makes a big display of kissing and cuddling them for show. The rest of the time they're being looked after by nannies. When her youngest was just two months old, Chrissie went and filmed abroad for fourteen weeks with only daily Skype calls as their contact.

Chrissie doesn't go anywhere without her entourage. There's always her hairdresser, make-up artist, personal fitness trainer and stylist on hand. Plus four bodyguards everywhere – even on a movie set. There are several people on the payroll. It's basically so that she has them at her beck and call for when she gets bored and wants to be entertained. Anyone who does the slightest thing to upset her is instantly fired, so you can imagine that her staff turnover is pretty high.

Nor does Chrissie think anything of holding up expensive shoots. I've often had to phone a photographer to tell him that she's 'on her way', knowing that she's decided to go off and do something else altogether. We'll battle with her, trying to dissuade her from going shopping or getting drunk with her friends in a restaurant so that she meets at least some of her obligations. The fact is, if it wasn't for her entourage, Chrissie's life would be totally out of control.

I suppose I shouldn't be ungrateful. Chrissie's life as a diva sees about forty people get a regular pay cheque, and that includes house-keepers, gardeners, drivers, accountants, publicists and so on. When Chrissie is up for a big role, she's far from alone in crossing her fingers that she gets it.

Chrissie gets asked to do a lot of charity work and she's got a reputation for being very generous with her time. She's done a lot for charities abroad and you'll see stories in the papers about her visits to children in hospital or AIDS victims in South Africa. I suppose the charities must be happy about this because there's always a lot of press attention and it must help with awareness. But if you looked closely, you'd realise that she doesn't work for any one charity for very long – quite simply, after she's made a few personal appearances, they don't ask her to do any more. That's because while she's in front of the cameras looking saintly in her floaty white dresses, behind the scenes there's always a drama.

Chrissie won't stay anywhere without her rider in place – not even in the middle of a desert, and believe me I should know. This includes, but is not restricted to: Diptyque candles; a floral arrange-ment of gardenias, jasmine and lilies; Cristal champagne; room-temperature Evian water; a masseuse; two full-length mirrors; fruit platter . . . you get the picture. When someone once dared to suggest that it was quite difficult and expensive for the charities to fulfil these riders, she exploded and said that she was saving them tens of thousands of pounds in personal appearance fees to provide them with acres of free publicity in the papers, so this was the least they could do.

Funnily enough, Chrissie quite often arranges the publicity at these charity events herself. And takes a fee from the magazine for doing

186

so. There isn't much that has happened in Chrissie's life that hasn't been captured for posterity. At one point, there was quite serious talk that she would film the birth of her youngest child for a reality TV show. It was only when someone pointed out that an elective caesarean might not be quite right for her earth-mother image that she decided against it. (Of course she had an elective caesarean – how else could she organise her film schedule around the birth? Let alone book the tummy tuck and boob lift that took place at the same time.)

The big problem right now is that Chrissie is getting older. She's not getting the parts she used to and her tantrums are getting worse. We all dread mornings – if she looks in the mirror and finds a wrinkle that wasn't there before, all hell breaks loose. Her plastic surgeon has warned her that he won't do more work on her. But she'll just find someone else to do it instead. At the moment you can't tell she's had much done – she tells her fans that she just drinks lots of water and has eight hours of sleep a night – mainly because of touch-up work that's done on any photo taken of her. But that's not going to work for much longer.

And worst of all, there are lots of people that Chrissie has screwed over on her way to the top. Her family don't speak to her anymore. She's rude to film crew (she screamed at a poor runner for bringing her Pepsi instead of Diet Cola and insisted the director sack him at once) and even the builders she hired to work on her latest country mansion have resigned halfway through the job, unable to take the abuse any longer. I've just had to take a phone call from a tabloid newspaper threatening to run a story from one of her co-stars about her behaviour on the last film set. So that's another cheque she's going to have to write. One day someone is going to speak out and we won't be able to do anything about it. When that day happens, I'll move to a war zone for some much-needed peace and quiet.

Susannah, 41, personal assistant to the stars

National surveys over the last forty years have consistently shown that, at any one time, two in every hundred Americans want to be famous.[47] I doubt whether the percentage is very different in the UK. One survey showed that 54 per cent of teens wanted to be famous (compared to just 15 per cent of them wanting a medical career)[48]; another found that even pre-teens are chasing the stars with 12 per cent wanting to be sportsmen, 11 per cent pop stars and 11 per cent actors.[49] Compare this to twenty-five years ago when the top three desirable careers were teaching, banking and medicine. The celebrity culture is one that has become particularly pervasive in the last decade with the rise and rise of reality TV, in which anyone can become famous just for 'being themselves'. No need for a specific talent or years of slogging on the small clubs circuit.

Of course, you don't have to be a psychopath to be a celebrity . . . but it helps! If someone wants to be famous, there are psychopathic traits that would make their rise quicker and easier. Lack of remorse or guilt means they can tread on others as effortlessly as walking on stepping stones in their climb to the top. Similarly, feelings of entitlement ensure that they never waver in their belief that they should be famous: no setback or criticism will make them falter. When Simon Cowell tells a psychopathic auditionee: 'If your lifeguard duties were as good as your singing, a lot of people would be drowning' – they are unfazed. They might even answer back that he is wrong.

Chrissie demonstrates other key temperaments: cultivating a public image that is at odds with her private behaviour; charming to those who are useful to her, awful to those who are not; easily prone to boredom; lack of empathy with even her own children; quick to throw a tantrum; multiple partners and marriages. These are all psychopathic traits, yes, but also traits we have known and loved-to-hate in divas over the years.

The question is: do you have to be psychologically damaged to want to be a celebrity or does it just turn some of them that way? There are certainly plenty of stories of famous stars described as being 'normal and nice' to begin with but who are then driven mad by the relentless pressure to be picture perfect all the time. Frequently, drugs are their chosen escape – and then they must suffer the consequences of serious addiction on top of everything else. Celebrities may feel that their lives are in the hands of strangers – their public, who may be adoring right now but could easily turn on them if they wear the wrong outfit, make a bad film or fall in love with someone their fans disapprove of. This pressure gets to them. A study of 100 stars across all fields – entertainers, sport, music – found that celebrities are four times more likely to kill themselves than the average American. In fact, the average age of death for celebrities overall was found to be fifty-eight, compared to an average of seventy-two for other Americans.[50]

There is even the 'Beckham Syndrome', a phenomena which has been nicknamed by psychologists – denoting those afflicted by it rather than describing the Beckhams themselves of course – for those who wish to become rich and famous without exercising any talent or effort. That desire in itself is borderline psychopathic, with its unrealistic goals and narcissistic entitlement.

Equally, there are stories of celebrities who acted as if they were famous before they were: stage school students putting on endless shows for their family and demanding an agent before they've even started school. But the prevalent stories are those of a celebrity's childhood that reveals early abandonment: the most common psychological explanation for wanting fame is to overcome early, traumatic rejection. After all – how can you say that no one loves you if tens of thousands of people in the stadium are singing along to your songs night after night or clapping and cheering your dramatic performance on the stage? Think of Marilyn Monroe and how her early rejection by her mother sent her on a lifelong path in which she sought public adoration and yet she was never sated or made happy by it.

Trying to assess whether a celebrity is a psychopath or psychologically damaged or whether fame and the life it brings is simply a side-effect of their talent can be as hard as trying to spot the difference between identical twins.

As to whether *your* celebrity crush is a psychopath . . . Well, he or she could be. But it is almost impossible to find out for certain, unless you get to know them very well. A psychopath can concoct an image to fool and manipulate their victims face to face. It's even easier for a celebrity to ensure that only the right face is presented to their adoring public. After all, they have a team of people working on their behalf to shape and protect their image, which is a commercial asset.

It's my belief, however, that the real sub-clinical psychopaths in the celebrity world are not so much the stars themselves as the puppet masters who create them. Especially those who control the reality TV shows.

THE SEVEN SIGNS OF A PSYCHOPATHIC CELEBRITY

Tony Hill began his career in television as a runner on a successful reality TV show. Although he was only tasked with fetching coffees for the crew and other menial chores, he was immediately absorbed by the job. Fresh out of media training, he relished the excitement of being on a hit programme. But even more than that, he was fascinated by the power the producers wielded over the contestants, often without them even realising. Tony worked there for four more series, getting promoted each time until he left in 2006 to work for Sleb Productions, a company that specialised in developing reality TV formats for sale around the world. He has become something of a minor celebrity himself, too, partly because his girlfriends are always 'stars' from the reality shows and partly because he has been a judge on a couple of talent programmes, honing a 'tough but fair' persona that everyone loves to hate.

By the time we meet Tony, he is the executive producer of a new show, *Heartbreak Island*, in which one man and ten women stay on an isolated tropical island and vie to become the winning couple. Their wedding takes place in the final episode and they receive a cash prize of £1 million. The catch? The women are all the man's ex-girlfriends.

Tony flies out to the exotic setting, taking with him a hand-picked crew, which includes several good-looking young girls as the runners. No one is particularly surprised that Tony disappears to the loo several times with one of them during the long flight. They do raise a collective eyebrow when he takes a different one off to the executive lounge while everyone is waiting for their luggage.

Before filming starts, Tony has a meeting with his director, editors and cameramen to discuss the script. This may be a reality TV show but Tony makes it clear that he's not leaving anything to chance. Each of the contestants is assigned a 'character', and the director will ensure that that is how they are portrayed. (The director is a little unsure about this approach but it's his first major break for the network – he's not going to say no to any of Tony's suggestions.) There's a gold-digger, a vamp, an innocent, a career girl and so on. Tony hasn't actually met any of the contestants but he's seen their audition tapes. Besides, he knows that he can manipulate them and edit the footage without too much trouble to get what he wants.

Sign 1 Tony's belief that he has the right to sleep with the crew, manipulate their ethics and act as supreme puppet master of the show's contestants demonstrates the psychopath's key characteristic of grandiosity.

In order to get the game going, Tony throws a big party the night before filming starts. But while his crew are served a non-alcoholic punch, the man at the centre of the series – Mark – and the ten ex-girlfriends are all given generous quantities of triple-shot cocktails. Tony then tells the runners to befriend the girls at the party and tell them rumours that they've heard: that Mark fancies another one; or that one of the girls has already cheated by sleeping with Mark the week before. All lies, of course. It has the desired effect and by the end of the night at least four of the girls have had a screaming, drunken row and Mark has snogged two others. When they begin filming the next day everyone is severely hungover and on edge.

Just to make it even more fun, Tony has told two of his cameramen that he needs to fire one of them but he hasn't decided which one yet. He then sits back and enjoys the bribes they each try to ply him with in order to keep their jobs.

Sign 2 By plying them with alcohol and deliberately inciting aggression and/or sex Tony is careless and manipulative when it comes to the wellbeing – mental or otherwise – of his crew and the contestants.

Tony needs big audience figures for this show – he's the executive producer and he wants to impress the network by making sure that he knocks any other programme in competition with his for six. By coincidence, one of his old colleagues is producing a gameshow on another channel, running at the same time. Tony takes great delight in texting him every week when he beats him in the ratings. In order to stay at the top spot Tony launches an aggressive PR campaign. As the contestants are safely hidden from the 'real world', he feeds the newspapers and magazines with stories about them. Having paid their 'friends' to spill the beans, he's managed to dig up some juicy dirt about some of the girls' past, complete with pictures. He also had some good stuff to work with based on the contestants' confidential statements: he told them he needed to know everything in order to properly assess their psychological health to take part in the show. So the girl who took an overdose when she discovered her father was not her real father will get an almighty shock when filming is over and she is shown interviews from the man formerly known as dad talking about her suicide attempts.

Sign 3 Tony shows a callous lack of responsibility towards his contestants.

After a few weeks, boredom sets in. Tony decides that the game isn't exciting enough – it needs more drama. He calls the women into the diary room one by one and tells one of them that he suspects Mark might be HIV positive; he tells another that her grandmother has died (this doesn't really add anything to the game but he is fascinated to see her reaction); yet another that she is being called fat by the press. He tells the rest that he thinks they're fabulous and that they are the most likely winner before revealing that one of the other women has cheated. Of course, he winks, you need to keep this to yourself. Then he tells the prop buyer to double the amount of alcohol supplied and sits back to watch the fireworks.

Sign 4 Like most psychopaths, Tony is prone to boredom. He relieves it here by trying out ever more extreme games on the contestants.

All the while, Tony is sleeping with several of the runners and telling each of them that they've 'got a real future' in television – particularly if they stick with him. Little do they know that the minute Tony lands back in the UK he'll delete their phone numbers from his mobile and they'll never hear from him again. The crew are in a state of panic as Tony suddenly and without bothering to inform anybody, sent both of the cameramen back home and two more needed to be flown out. He decided to evict one of the female players mid-week, involving expensive last minute edits and changes to the scheduled programme simply because he 'felt like it'. The director has daily meetings with Tony and these are sending him to the edge of a nervous breakdown – one day Tony will be thrilled with how the programme is going, the very next day he has an explosive tantrum about how terrible it is.

Signs 5 and 6 Tony's decisions lack any forethought or consideration of the consequences for his unfortunate production team. It is only down to their frantic worth that *Heartbreak Island* avoids an embarrasing on-air disaster. Tony's random and epic temper tantrums are evidence of the psychopath's psycho style, he will just as quickly calm down and then behave as if nothing has happened.

When the series comes to an end the winning couple are unhappily married. They also discover that complicated legal matters tie up their million-pound cash prize – it takes a year to come through and they don't get the full amount (the small print dictates that fees and costs are to be deducted). Two of the contestants have to go straight into an alcohol rehab programme, three of the runners believe they are having an exclusive affair with Tony and one is being treated for sex addiction. The rest of the contestants are forced into hiding when they get home and see the slurs that have been printed in the papers about them – one was accused of discrimination towards those with HIV and flees the country, the vilification is so extreme.

Tony? Tony laughs all the way to the bank and commissions series two.

Sign 7 Tony has not a shred of remorse or guilt. And why would he? No psychopath ever said 'sorry' sincerely. He flies home with not a care in the world.

MIRROR, MIRROR ON THE WALL, WHO'S THE MOST NARCISSISTIC OF ALL?

A study found that celebrities scored higher on the Narcissistic Personality Inventory (NPI) than either a control group of MBA students or the general populace.[51] Furthermore, it found that female celebrities were significantly more narcissistic than their male counterparts, which is the opposite of findings in the population at large.

Of these celebrities, the most narcissistic were reality TV stars (comedians, actors and musicians followed behind in succession). Those, possibly, who believe they should be famous just for 'being themselves'.

The authors also found that even years of experience in the entertainment industry had no effect on NPI scores, suggesting that the celebrities have narcissistic tendencies before they become famous.

THE STANFORD PRISON EXPERIMENT – THE BLUEPRINT FOR REALITY TV?

In 1971 an experiment was carried out to study the psychological effects of becoming a prisoner or prison guard. The researchers essentially wanted to know whether problems caused in prisons were a consequence of the situation itself (i.e. being in prison) or of the guards' personalities. The results of the experiment and the conclusions drawn are very controversial but there are some parallels with reality television frameworks.

Psychology professor Dr Phillip Zimbardo of Stanford University, USA, conducted the experiment. Seventy-five male undergraduates applied to take part in the programme, of whom twenty-four were chosen (they were deemed the most psychologically stable). Some were randomly appointed as 'guards', the rest as 'prisoners'. The prisoners were given numbers instead of names and wore uncomfortable clothing and chains round their ankles. Guards were given a khaki uniform, mirrored sunglasses and wooden batons to wear round their waists.

The guards were told by Zimbardo that the prisoners were to have instilled in them a sense of boredom, fear 'to some degree', that their lives were controlled by the guards and that they had no privacy. 'That is, in this situation, we'll have all the power and they'll have none.'

The experiment was due to last two weeks. In the event, it was called off abruptly after just six days. One third of the guards displayed genuine 'sadistic' tendencies. Prisoners suffered and accepted this brutal treatment and humiliation. They had their mattresses taken away from them and had to sleep on concrete floors; some were stripped naked as punishment; one was locked in a closet as 'solitary confinement'. Zimbardo himself became too embroiled in the extreme scenarios and it was only when his girlfriend visited on the sixth day that she complained that it had gone too far. No one else present had been able to see it.

The conclusion drawn was that the *situation* caused the behaviour of the guards and the prisoners rather than anything inherent in their own personalities. This suggests that even the most mild-mannered of people could become sadistic guards, given the right circumstances.

However, this conclusion has since been questioned. It would no longer be ethically acceptable to repeat this experiment exactly as before, but similar research has not produced the same results. Yet despite the fact that the Stanford prison experiment was universally condemned and is never to be repeated, is it just me or have we seen things on TV that bear a close resemblance recently?

Top ten movie psychos
Robert Carlyle as Begbie in *Trainspotting*
Joe Pesci as Tommy DeVito in *Goodfellas*
Anthony Hopkins as Hannibal Lecter in *Silence of the Lambs*
Jack Nicholson as Jack Torrance in *The Shining*
Christian Bale as Patrick Bateman in *American Psycho*
Kathy Bates as Annie Wilkes in *Misery*
Renee Zellweger as Roxie Hart in *Chicago*
Robert Mitchum as Max Cady in *Cape Fear*
Bette Davis as Baby Jane Hudson in *Whatever Happened to Baby Jane?*
Glenn Close as Alex Forrest in *Fatal Attraction*

SIMON COWELL – PERPETRATOR OF A PSYCHO-PATHIC SOCIETY?

Let's be clear: I'm not calling Simon Cowell a psychopath (although he appears to call himself one – his company is called SyCo: a play on words or double bluff?). No, my charge against Cowell is that his hit TV shows *The X Factor* and *Britain's Got Talent* (with Stateside versions of both these programmes) could be said to contribute to a psychopathic society; a society that supports psychopathic maxims in its encouragement of shallow displays of emotion, the pursuit of fortune and glory and competitions won as much by manipulation as by skill. A recent article by Professor David Wilson tore into the macci-nations behind *The X Factor*, in which 'ordinary' people compete to win a million-pound recording contract.[51] Wilson's point is that the idea that a show like this portrays any kind of 'reality' is now a lie: 'The programme has descended into a grotesque puppet show, with Cowell acting as the cynical puppeteer, pulling the strings of the contestants and the heart strings of the viewers.'

Wilson is in a position to recognise the problem. He worked briefly as an advisor on *Big Brother* and draws parallels with the show's cancellation after 'its slide into self-parody'.

Cowell is accused of whipping up an hysterical atmosphere, with the different contestants being given 'characters' they have to play: the villains, the hard-luck victims and so on. In fact, there is 'an absurd amount of histrionic self-regard' among the contestants, says Wilson, 'such as when we hear some 17-year-old proclaiming: "I've been fighting for this all my life," as if preparing for the D-Day landings.'

Cowell, of course, is not alone in operating the machina-tions of shows like this. But he is the most visible and it is the curiosity of his desire to both be famous and bring others to fame – in other words, to do all he can to encourage psycho-pathic characteristics in society – that merits the attention I have given him here.

THE INFLUENCE OF CELEBRITIES ON YOUNG MINDS

The following statistics were picked out by the website www.pinkstinks.co.uk as part of its campaign to fight back against the media obsession with women who are rich, famous and thin and therefore presented as role models to the younger generation.

- 35 per cent of girls chose Victoria Beckham as the celebrity having the greatest influence, with Leona Lewis at 32 per cent and Kate Moss and Amy Winehouse in third and fourth place.[53]

- 37 per cent of teachers said their pupils just wanted to be famous for the sake of being famous.

- More than 70 per cent of teachers believed that celebrity culture is perverting children's aspirations and expectations and is producing a generation who do not believe education and hard work are necessary to achieve financial success.

- 44 per cent said that their pupils tried to emulate the role models through their looks and behaviour, with 32 per cent modelling themselves on Paris Hilton.[54]

THE ETHICS OF REALITY TELEVISION PRODUCERS

Richard Crew is a former documentary producer in Los Angeles who closed his production company to become a media scholar. During his studies he decided to examine reality gaming and dating shows, and interviewed former employees and producers to find out what ethical principles producers apply when creating 'reality' television.[55]

His questions were framed by the ethical concerns he considered important in reality TV: that non-professional participants are treated in a 'fair and responsible manner', and that the stories of ordinary people and their experiences are presented 'in an ethical manner'.

Crew points out that there are serious consequences for failing to adhere to these concerns, especially for psychologically unsuited participants. In 1997, the first contestant evicted from *Expedition Robinson*, the Swedish inspiration for *Survivor*, threw himself under a train.

Crew discovered in the course of his research that while the executive producers would be careful to say that there were measures in place to ensure fair and responsible treatment, 'when I talked with the production personnel below the executive producer level, I heard a different story'.

A supervising producer and story editor claimed that no ethical direction had been given to them. Rather, 'they were directed to "create entertaining stories"'. They claimed that this pressure came from the networks; 'specifically, network representatives insist that reality shows be "cast" with characters who, when put together, will create conflict'.

Crew also found that alcohol is frequently made freely available, 'significantly affecting' the behaviour of the participants. A producer admitted that a lot of footage with slurred speech was cut. Producers can also heighten drama during the editing process; one story editor said this 'cheating footage' was necessary because 'cast members don't always demonstrate on camera how they really feel'. There is also an editing technique employed known as the 'Franken bite'; this is deemed acceptable 'if it depicts the character's point of view'. It is when a participant's words from different days are creatively edited to make it seem as if they were cut from a single scene.

Crew concluded that ethical standards to protect the psychological wellbeing of cast members are in place. 'But since producers are required to make a myriad of decisions during the production process, it is surprising they mostly operate without ethical direction from their superiors.' The networks want entertainment, 'so the opportunity exists for an individual's ethical standards to be crowded out by pragmatic considerations for audience stimulation and successful ratings'.

SUMMARY AND ADVICE

The question we have pondered in this chapter is whether one can tell the difference between a psychopathic celebrity and a 'normal' celebrity. Both often display delusions of grandeur, overbearing egos, a belief that they are at the centre of everyone's world and a ruthless will to succeed. Without getting close to the celebrity, it may be impossible ever to tell.

At least while your celebrity crush remains at a safe distance there is no immediate danger to you even if they are psychopathic.

The most narcissistic celebrities are reality TV stars. One wonders, however, whether these 'stars' are not merely toys in the hands of puppet masters. Are they really verging on the psychopathic or just portrayed that way? Audiences are becoming increasingly immune to 'shocking' television and the networks are having to work harder to create programmes with any real conflict or drama in their bid to win the ratings war; this means that their contestants are subjected to ever more outrageous manipulations.

There is, perhaps, a further lurking menace in that celebrities are increasingly revered in today's society; their influence as role models could not only create little monsters who are following their every move, but they may be contributing to increasingly psychopathic values and behaviours in society generally. In this kind of society, narcissism is seen as normal, histrionic emotions are displayed whenever someone suffers the slightest setback and other people are used and abused merely as means to an end. The psychologist Oliver James posits something similar in his book *Affluenza*, in which he says that what he calls selfish capitalism is a virus-like condition that is spreading through the more affluent economies.[56] In these countries, people define themselves through their wealth and also by other superficial values – how attractive and famous they are and how much they can show these things off.

To combat this, he recommends that we try to look 'inward' rather than 'outward', watch less television, involve ourselves in the family unit more and try not to see life as a competition. It's simple stuff but I think it works. Your best defence against a psychopath is a constant check on your own values: if someone is persuading you to bend or even break your moral code, then they are not the right person to have in your life. Even if they are off the telly.

10

ARE YOU A PSYCHOPATH?

The good news is that, by definition, if you think you are a psychopath, you are almost certainly not one. However, there are times in everyone's life when we may be driven to psychopathic behaviour, to become what we call a 'situational psychopath'. Perhaps someone bullied at school will be driven to take excessive, aggressive revenge. Or perhaps a lover spurned you and you want to make them feel the pain of your hurt. At these times, you may experience the single-minded ruthlessness of a psychopath.

But to be a true psychopath you must have enduring psychopathic traits that manifest themselves across time and contexts. A psychopath is not provoked by a particular event nor are they later ashamed or apologetic for their earlier actions.

When I look back on the months running up to my wedding day, I want to cry with shame. To be honest, I don't know how I actually went through with it – the girl I fell in love with and asked to marry me disappeared somewhere between the proposal and the honeymoon. By the time we were on the flight home she was back to her normal self again, although I was left feeling pretty scarred. I think she feels embarrassed herself but we don't talk about that terrible time – I'd rather not remember what she's capable of.

It started from the moment we tried to fix a date. She already had three preferred venues – which was news to me as we'd only been seeing each other for a year and neither of us had mentioned marriage before I proposed – and none of them were available in less than six months' time. So she called one up and said that her father had had a heart attack recently and unless she had the wedding soon, she feared he wouldn't be able to walk her down the aisle. Which was half-true – he'd had a heart scare, but there was certainly no talk of him having only a few months to live. Anyway, she did a good sob story and they found a Friday afternoon for us, which was the next best thing.

Then when it came to drawing up the guest list, she told me that I couldn't invite some of my friends and even some of my family. She said it was because we were limited on numbers. But there was room for 250 guests – I know she just thought some of my pals might drink too much or start a fight or something, although they hardly ever do.

With her bridesmaids, she was horrendous. She told one to lose two stone before the wedding day and another to dye her hair blonde. She picked out dresses that were expensive but hideously unflattering on them, making herself look better. The ultimate insult? She insisted they pay for the dresses as their wedding present.

Choosing the dress of her dreams was, inevitably, a nightmare – even I started waking up in sweats thinking about French Chantilly lace and pearl buttons. There were endless appointments with bridal shops and dressmakers, the living room had piles of bride magazines everywhere and her mother took on a permanently panicked ashen look. At least four times she said she had absolutely, finally decided on a dress; her parents would pay for the material and seamstress and then after two or three fittings she would go off it and sob that she had to go and find another.

We went to a very high-end department store to register our wedding list. I had to leave halfway through as we had a screaming row. She wouldn't look at anything below £100 and most things were around the £250 mark. She even had a couple of things that were a few thousand pounds, saying that I had some rich relatives who 'ought to stump up'. Naturally, these were the few on my side who were invited, even though they aren't close. Funnily enough, in the months running up to our wedding they were suddenly being invited over for cosy suppers and she even dropped hints that when we had a baby, they would be asked to be godparents. I know they would have found this odd – we barely knew their names this time last year.

When she found out that another of her friends was having a hen night close to hers, she had hysterical fits over the phone to her matron of honour until the date was changed. She even spread the rumour that her friend's fiancé was cheating on her: she wanted their wedding called off so that she didn't have to share any of the limelight. Luckily, her friend was wise to it and the ploy didn't work.

She also dictated most of the details of her hen party, including how much money everyone was expected to contribute and that she wanted a book full of photos and messages from friends who weren't even coming to the wedding. When one friend said she couldn't come to the hen night because she was pregnant and it would be very near her due date, she cajoled on the phone for an hour until her friend broke down and agreed to be there.

The night before the wedding we had the rehearsal, and I got very close to calling the whole thing off. She was screaming at her brides-maids that they 'weren't walking properly' and we were all ruining 'her' wedding. Even her father got shouted at for not wearing the right tie to the family dinner that night.

At no point was I ever asked what I would like at the wedding – not the venue, the food, the flowers or the music. I know that it's an important day for a bride – but isn't it my day a bit, too?

In the end the day itself was not too bad. She was a little hyster-ical during the photos – it took three hours to get all the different set-ups she wanted and she had hair and make-up on standby throughout. When we had our first dance she was whispering in my ear: not sweet

nothings but dance step instructions. At least she was OK with the
speeches but that was only because she'd already had us all tell them
to her beforehand.

By the time she threw the bouquet to the cheering crowd – of
course it was pre-arranged who would catch it – I was smiling and
laughing like a demented clown. I was just so relieved that it was all
over and we could get back to normal again.

John, 32, newlywed

The bride-to-be in our story is certainly a strong candidate for the 'Bridezilla' tag – and she's far from being the only one. Weddings can be stressful occasions and are a good example of when you are more likely to become a 'situational psychopath', stressed by the competing demands placed on you. Not to mention that you are highly invested in a successful outcome. But while our bride's behaviour is borderline, she is still not a psychopath.

The word 'psycho' has become a catch-all phrase for any aggressive or bizarre behaviour that we don't understand. Who among us hasn't talked of a 'psycho boss' or 'psycho ex'? And even the most well-behaved citizens among us will have told a lie or two, or broken the rules to suit our own ends. Given the right set of circumstances any one of us can temporarily act like a psychopath – but that is very far from actually *being* a psychopath. To be a psychopath, you really do have to be very, very bad indeed.

But what is it like to actually be a psychopath? Do they mind being called one? I've known some to be quite happy with the label, proud of being somehow 'special' in a way. One or two have been indignant – those tend to be the ones who are in total denial about everything they have ever done. With no insight into their own condition they will fail to take any personal responsibility for their actions to the point of absolute denial even when confronted with clear evidence of their behaviour. 'I wasn't there,' they'll say. 'It wasn't me, guv,' is the refrain.

Most diagnosed psychopaths seem to find it rather fascinating and might even go and research the subject. But they don't have the emotional response you might expect; they couldn't care less about the negative connotations associated with the word. Generally, most psychopaths have little insight into their condition: they have never experienced anything else and therefore assume everyone is just the same. We do – and this is why it can be hard for society to handle psychopaths. We simply can't understand or believe that there are human beings who do not feel love, sorrow or guilt.

I have had a psychopath or two who has cottoned on to the fact that other people think that they are 'odd'. But they still wouldn't really care until it stops them from getting what they want (usually parole). I once asked a lecturer and well-known psychologist if he thought he was a psychopath. He beamed and said, 'Yes, I guess so – everybody asks me that.'

The good news for anyone around psychopaths is that their most acute rule-breaking and aggressive behaviours tend to settle down after the age of around forty.[57] On their part, the good news for them is that while they are not what you would call happy creatures, they tend not to suffer from anxiety or depression. In fact, as a psychopath, you might even be one of the world's more successful people – a leading politician, perhaps, or CEO of a bank? A cult leader?

The bad news for psychopaths is that they tend to be highly self-destructive. They will sabotage themselves almost as much as the people around them unless they are one of the more 'fortunate' ones who have managed to control and mask themselves better, finding roles in society where their psychopathic traits are an asset.

As we have seen throughout the book, there is no such thing as an average psychopath: they come in all guises. However, it might be worth looking at a psychopathic 'everyman' – one who is born of an unexceptional background yet goes on to display exceptional, chilling, characteristics.

Barry comes from a pretty average, working-class, no-frills kind of background. His mum and dad did their best but Barry began truanting from school from the age of ten. He fell in with a bad crowd and was soon a vandal on the local estates, sniffing glue and swigging cider. There was even a short stint in care when his parents lost control of him altogether. All Barry remembers of this time is quite enjoying the fact that his parents were tormented by his antics.

Sign 1 Barry is being brought up in pretty much the same manner as hundreds of thousands of other small boys with parents who are doing their best to care for him. Yet early on he has severe behavioural problems, which are typical of a budding psychopath.

Barry's existence as he grows up continues to be aimless. He does a bit of bar work but is sacked from most jobs for failing to turn up after one or two weeks. Not wanting to spend the little money he has on rent and not seeing why he should pay anything when he can get someone else to, Barry stays on his latest friend's sofas, drifting from place to place. Occasionally he commits petty crimes, stealing money from his mates or bottles of vodka from the local off-licence.

Sign 2 Psychopaths do not have goals – they drift from one activity to the next, doing whatever is necessary to survive, whether that is legal or not, moral or not.

Barry appears to make friends quite easily but they are dropped suddenly, without knowing why. In fact, he can't really distinguish between friends and acquaintances – they're all the same to him. He doesn't maintain contact with people who help him out and he can't understand why they don't seem pleased to see him when he shows up at their door at 3 a.m. after four years.

There's no proper girlfriend. If he does manage to reel someone in, he never holds onto her for long. 'Can't understand what bloody women want,' he'll mutter. He doesn't see why they should object to his suggestion that he'll give them beer and cigarettes if they have sex with him.

Sign 3 Barry has just enough charm to make friends but no ability to maintain a friendship. Without emotional stability or empathy he fails to understand other people; for him, they are there to serve his own purposes.

Barry falls out, argues or somehow comes into conflict with others all the time. He is known in various areas for taking offence easily and having explosive outbursts over trivial matters. Naturally, many people have learnt to cross over to the other side of the street if they see him approaching or harbour resentments about the last time Barry lost his rag with them. But, of course, it's never his fault. In fact, he can't understand why the world is so unkind to him. He thinks that he must be really unlucky.

Sign 4 Psychopaths see no link between their own actions and the consequences; they are completely without the ability to accept responsibility. More than that, the bad things that do happen to them are seen as 'bad luck'. Psychopaths therefore often feel disgruntled for themselves.

One night, Barry decides that he's had enough. The world owes him something, he thinks, and he is going to get it. First of all he steals a credit card from the wallet of the person whose sofa he is staying on that week and uses that card to try a spot of online gambling. Having lost hundreds of pounds on the card he then grabs some cash that he knows they have hidden in a tin in the kitchen cupboard, their savings for his summer holiday.

The cash is used to fund a long afternoon at the pub, punctuated by a quick visit to the local brothel. Afterwards, as Barry is walking along the street, he sees someone homeless begging for money. Barry kicks him in the stomach. A woman sees Barry do this and shouts at him and threatens to call the police. Barry stares at her, then just shrugs his shoulders and carries on.

When he gets back to the flat, he finds his friend distraught and searching for the missing money. Barry tells him that he thinks his friend's ex-girlfriend must have taken it – she popped round earlier that day (of course, she hadn't). Before the friend can discover that this isn't true, Barry has left.

Sign 5 Despite the fact that his friend has been giving him a place to stay, Barry has no respect for his friend's feelings, let alone his friend's money. Kicking the homeless man and blaming the ex-girlfriend for the theft are just further symptoms of Barry's callous disregard for others.

Barry is completely unrepentant about his highly immoral and mean behaviour. He finds the responses of people, such as the woman in the street, puzzling but also sort of interesting. There's a moment in the film *Malice*, starring Nicole Kidman, where she watches a mother in distress over injuries her child has suffered and then goes home to practise making the same sad faces in the mirror. That's pretty much how Barry feels.

Sign 6 Psychopaths have no remorse for the nasty things they do. They feel so little, in fact, that the emotions they see others display become a source of fascination for them. Think of how you feel when watching a wildlife programme: that's fairly similar to how a psychopath feels when watching you.

As it becomes increasingly obvious to those around him that Barry just doesn't 'get it' about his fellow human beings, that he isn't feeling what they express, he begins to get called 'a psychopath'. Again, he finds this interesting. He does a little research into the term, thinking that perhaps this will explain why the world is so unforgiving (he has always felt different . . . it would be nice to be something special). When he – inevitably – ends up in prison for fraud, Barry requests to be seen by the prison psychologist. He wishes to discuss his 'special needs' as a psychopath. The psychologist is professional and on his guard but finds Barry exceptionally persuasive. It's not long before he has arranged for Barry to get privileges within the prison system – such as lessons in car mechanics and extra visiting rights. Like many psychopaths before him, Barry will amass an extensive and colourful criminal record. He will end his sorry days in and out of prisons and bail hostels.

Sign 7 Despite the fact that Barry is a known criminal, the psychologist is taken in by Barry's manipulative charms. He's certainly not the first – even Robert Hare has fallen victim to an incarcerated client[58] – and he won't be the last. Manipulation is the psychopath's art of survival; it's hardly surprising that they are highly skilled at it.

THE VIGILANTE WHO 'ARRESTED' TEENAGERS

The *Daily Telegraph* reported in September 2010 on Anthony Sacks, twenty, a man who became so 'fed up' with youths loitering in his neighbourhood late at night that he got himself a police uniform, handcuffs and an earpiece radio and pretended to pound the beat.

Over two months, he handcuffed and detained several children on 'charges', including under-age smoking and 'being out late at night'. One fourteen-year-old was driven home, where Sacks lectured the mother for an hour on the dangers of tobacco. Another boy, aged fifteen, was taken home, where he warned the parents about their son being out late at night. On other occasions, Sacks handcuffed a boy for 'loitering' and ordered him to his car; he was let go after the boy shouted to someone he knew. He also used flashing lights on his car to stop a seventeen-year-old motorist.

Eventually, a mother of one of his 'suspects' became suspicious and asked for his ID. At Manchester crown court, Sacks pleaded guilty to false imprisonment, kidnapping and fraud. He was ordered to be detained under the Mental Health Act after a psychiatrist said he suffered from a personality disorder.

Sacks might appear to be a 'situational psychopath', driven to extreme measures by antisocial youths, although his diagnosis suggests that his strange behaviour was part of a more persistent dysfunction on his part. It is a reasonable guess that at least one of his victims might have privately referred to him as a 'psycho'. I suspect that he may have Obsessive–Compulsive Personality Disorder (the key features of which are a pervasive pattern of preoccupation with orderliness, perfectionism and mental and interpersonal control) with a good dose of grandiosity. It is also the case that a psychopath is more likely to join in with the ASBO crowd than to become a one-man police force. I include the story here as a cautionary tale: not everyone with grandiose and bizarre behaviour is necessarily a psychopath.

MISTAKING PSYCHOPATHY FOR AUTISM

Autism is a pervasive developmental disorder, a lifelong disability which affects a person's social understanding and ability to communicate. Like psychopathy, autism is a 'hidden' and poorly diagnosed condition. Yet it is remarkably prevalent: The National Autistic Society estimates that one in 100 people suffer from it (the same occurrence as psychopathy).

People with autism, particularly the less severe forms, can be unfairly castigated as psychopathic. It could be argued that autistic people and psychopaths are similar: after all, both can appear indifferent, lack a true empathetic appreciation of others' inner experience and are uninhibited by normal social rules. But where autistic people tend to withdraw socially (the word autism comes from the Greek term for 'self' or 'alone'), psychopaths can learn to attract and fascinate their peers. In that sense they are at completely opposite ends of the dysfunctional spectrum.

Both autism and psychopathy has been linked to abnormalities in amygdala functioning.[59] The amygdala is a one-inch-long, almond-shaped structure that sits in the temporal lobe just a little distance from either ear. Although small, it is 'critical in regulating emotion and in guiding emotion-regulated behaviours'.[60] Some of what it does is to facilitate learning from consequences and recognising facial expression. But although it is the same area of the brain that is affected for both autistics and psychopaths, the type of impairment seems very different.

We know that psychopaths fail to learn from punishment and they can fail to 'read' certain facial expressions in others but when shown a series of photographs of faces and asked to make a judgement regarding how trustworthy that person is, they can do it.[61] People with autism are the opposite way around: they are able to learn from punishment and reward but cannot distinguish between trustworthy and untrustworthy faces.[62]

PSYCHOPATHS AND ANXIETY

Hervey Cleckley originally noted 'absence of nervousness' in the psychopaths he studied.[63] Psychopaths by and large have reduced anxiety levels,[64] particularly those who demonstrate more psychopathic personality traits – the type we are largely discussing in this book – than lifestyle characteristics.[65]

When a psychopath does report anxiety, it is not really clear what he or she might actually be feeling, as all emotions seem to have a different meaning and are experienced differently by psychopaths. It isn't that they don't have any emotions at all; but they are believed to be 'proto-emotions'.[66] Proto-emotions are shallow, rapid and short-lived responses to immediate circumstances. Psychopaths are not particularly likely to worry or even ruminate for any prolonged period. Must be quite nice really.

Anxiety is a big part of what inhibits us from illegal or immoral behaviour – it can be thought of as a key ingredient of our conscience. Psychopaths don't have this problem so don't feel apprehensive when contemplating or carrying out a nasty deed.

PSYCHOPATHY AND DRUG ABUSE

Psychopaths are significantly more likely to meet the diagnostic criteria for alcohol dependency and drug dependency (particularly where lots of different types of drugs are used by one individual).

This is most likely in psychopaths who lead chaotic lifestyles; so those psychos who are successful at blending in aren't as likely to have substance abuse disorders (although they won't be averse to the odd pill popping or powder snorting on a recreational or reckless thrill basis).[67]

Most worryingly, psychopathic drug users are more likely than others to risk sharing needles.[68]

QUIZ: HOW PSYCHOPATHIC ARE YOU?

1. You are in a queue and someone pushes in front of you. How do you react?

    A) Tut to yourself but say nothing.

    B) Grab them by the scruff of the neck and tell them to push off.

    C) Start chatting to them like a long lost friend.

2. Do you think the country would be better off if you were running it?

    A) Maybe.

    B) Yes.

    C) No.

3. You have been told that you will receive an electric shock if you eat another chocolate biscuit. How do you feel?

    A) A bit scared and decide against reaching out for another.

B) Absolutely nothing and try to grab two this time.

C) Utterly terrified and sit on your hands.

4.   **You go to the funeral of a young teenager who has died in a car accident. How do you feel?**

A) Very sad for the poor family and friends.

B) Fascinated by the reactions of everyone there – you commit the looks on their faces to memory and practise imitating them when you get home.

C) Totally heartbroken – you are the last to leave, dragged sobbing from the church.

5.   **Your attitude to drugs is:**

A) You can take 'em or leave 'em.

B) Try anything once – once a weekend, that is.

C) They are all highly dangerous and addictive – you would never touch anything.

6.   **It's your first anniversary with your spouse. How do you decide to mark the occasion?**

A) You book a weekend at the European city you went to for your honeymoon.

B) You forget about it and spend the night with your lover.

C) You book the church so you can renew your vows.

7.   **As a teenager, did you ever commit any crimes?**

A) Not really – perhaps you stole some sweets from the corner shop.

B) Are you kidding? You were on first-name terms with the local police they had cautioned you so often.

C) Are you kidding? You were a prefect at school – you had to set an example.

8. **At work you have been asked to put together a presentation for the following day. Your response is:**

A) To call the team together and ask everyone to pull their weight and make this happen.

B) To tell your assistant to do it and then go off for a long lunch.

C) To stay up all night, drinking strong coffee and sweating blood over it. But you get it done.

9. **Your friend gets an expensive watch that you really want. What do you do?**

A) Look online to see if you can get a cheap deal and buy one.

B) Steal it.

C) Fawn over it and acknowledge to yourself that you will never earn enough to get one.

10. **When driving your car, how fast do you go?**

A) Fast enough to have earned three points on your licence but on the whole you stay within the speed limits.

B) As fast as you possibly can, flashing other drivers to get out of your way – and that's just on the side streets.

C) An average of 20 m.p.h. but you'd really rather take the bus.

How did you do?

Mostly A's: You're pretty normal – sometimes capable of being selfish but generally a good guy.

Mostly B's: You're bordering on the psychopathic. You can't have many friends. Then again, what do you care?

Mostly C's: You're certainly no psychopath but you are very sensitive. Be careful that you don't allow people to walk all over you.

(Please note – this is *not* a diagnostic tool, it's just for fun, besides if you were a psychopath, you would lie all the way through it anyway.)

PSYCHOPATHIC PLEASURE

When psychopaths find something that interests them, they will get tunnel vision, ignoring extraneous details. This can be both an advantage and a disadvantage. The drawback is that it makes them particularly insensitive to peripheral 'threat cues' and they may therefore miss things in their environment that are warnings.[69] Hare has noticed how psychopathic fighter pilots were lauded for their fearless attacks on the enemy – but they would undo themselves ultimately by failing to take note of unexciting things such as fuel levels or the positions of other planes.[70]

Of course, we all focus onto things that are enjoyable to some extent but psychopaths can take it to an extreme.[71] They may pursue pleasure aggressively, but given their impoverished emotional capacity, their lives are likely to be no more, if not less, satisfied than most. Perhaps concentrating on the exciting things in life (or just 'feeling' less) is good for the psychopath's mental health however – those with high scores on the Psychopathy Checklist tend to experience less symptoms of depression.[72]

SUMMARY AND ADVICE

If you've read this book and worried that you might be a psychopath, the good news is that you are probably not one. A true psychopath almost certainly wouldn't recognise himself as one – they don't see themselves as 'bad' – and even if they did, they wouldn't worry about it.

The key thing to remember is that while we can all behave psychopathically in certain situations, the point about true psychopathy is that it is enduring and consistent. Ticking off just one or two of the psychopathic traits we've explored isn't enough – you must display a whole cluster of symptoms. Furthermore, it isn't the badness of a particular act that is important but your characteristic ways of relating to people. Being a murderer is horrific but it doesn't necessarily make you a psychopath; in fact, you can be a psychopath without even breaking the law.

Psychopaths are not insane; they do not hallucinate or carry out vicious acts because voices in their head told them to. Indeed, they are fully aware of what they do and in reasonable control of their behaviour. They have no internal conflict, no conscience: so if you've ever felt remorse or sorrow over a horrible thing that you've done, you are not a psychopath.

Of course, there are times where we may be driven to psychopathic behaviour. Any time where we feel under intense pressure may cause psychopathic-like tunnel vision in our desire to get what we need or want – from the perfect wedding day to revenge on a bully. Again, while the resulting behaviour may be regrettable, it is not psychopathic. We are redeemable.

If you are a psychopath, you may be lucky enough to be one of life's success stories. With no moral compass you will be ruthless in your pursuit of reward and pleasure. A psychopath is less likely than others to suffer depression, is unlikely to feel much anxiety and certainly doesn't worry himself about the feelings of others. This makes for a comparatively stress-free existence. The only comforting factor for others is that you will begin to 'mellow' somewhat in middle age.

On the other hand, an average psychopath will most often have little stability in his life, and with constant fights and fallings out with those around him may well feel that he is 'unlucky' and picked on. Psychopaths are also self-sabotaging and any equilibrium achieved will be quickly shattered. Unable to fit into societal norms, a reasonably perceptive psychopath is likely to feel 'different' and unfairly sidelined from those around him. While you may envy a thriving psychopath for, say, his ability to single-mindedly pursue riches, you can take consolation in the knowledge that he will not experience any profundity of happiness no matter how many gold bricks have built his house.

NOTES

1. R. D. Hare, *Without Conscience: The Disturbing World of the Psychopaths Among Us* (New York: Guilford Press, 1998).
2. J. R. Weisz and C. J. McCarty, 'Can we trust parents' reports on cultural and ethnic differences in child psychopathology?', *Journal of Abnormal Psychology* 108 (1999): 598-605.
3. D. J. Cooke, C. Michie, S. D. Hart and D. Clark, 'Assessing psychopathy in the UK: concerns about cross-cultural generalisability', *British Journal of Psychiatry* 186 (2005): 339-345.
4. D. J. Cooke and C. Michie, 'Psychopathy across cultures: North America and Scotland compared', *Journal of Abnormal Psychology* 108 (1999): 58-68.
5. Judith Rawnsley, *Going for Broke: Nick Leeson and the Collapse of Barings Bank* (1996)
6. *ibid.*
7. B. J. Board and K Fritzon, 'Disordered Personalities at Work', *Psychology, Crime and Law* 11(1) (2005): 17-32
8. G. K. Levenston, C. J. Patrick, M. M. Bradley and P. J. Lang, 'The psychopath as observer: emotion and attention in picture processing', *Jounal of Abnormal Psychology*, 109 (2006): 373–385.
9. R. D. Hare, 'Electrodermal and cardiovascular correlates of psychopathy' in R. D. Hare and D. Schalling

(eds), *Psychopathic Behaviour: Approaches to Research* (Chicester, England: John Wiley & Sons, 1978), 107-144.

10. Charles-Albert Poissant, *How to Think Like a Millionaire* (London: Thorsons, 1989).

11. Erin Arvedlund, *Madoff: The Man Who Stole $65 Billion* (London: Penguin, 2009).

12. Jon Kelly, 'The Strange Allure of Robert Maxwell', BBC News Website, 4 May 2007.

13. *ibid*.

14. Published on the PriceWaterhouseCooper website: www.pwc.com.

15. S. Schachter, *The Psychology of Affiliation: Experimental Studies of the Sources of Gregariousness* (Stanford, CA: Stanford University Press, 1959).

16. R. D. Hare and B. Gilstrom, 'Hand gestures and speech encoding difficulties in psychopaths', unpublished manuscript (1997).

17. A. Raine, M. O'Brian, N. Smiley, A. Scerbo and Chan, 'Reduced lateralisation in verbal dichotic listening in adolescent psychopaths', *Journal of Abnormal Psychology* 99 (1990). R.D. Also Hare and J. Julai, 'Psychopathy and Cerebal asymmetry in semantic processing, *Personality and Individual Differences* 9 (1998): 328–37

18. S. M. Louth *et al.*, 'Acoustic distinctions in the speech of male psychopaths', *Journal of Psycholinguistic Research* 27 (1998): 375-384.

19. Karen Karbo, 'Friendship: The Laws of Attraction,' *Psychology Today* (November 2006).

20. 'Love at First Fright' was a report in which participants at two theme parks in Texas were asked to look at a photograph of a man or woman and rate their attractiveness. Those who had just climbed off a roller-coaster found them significantly more attractive. C. M. Meston

and P. F. Frohlich, 'Love at First Fright: Partner salience moderates roller coaster-induced excitation transfer', *Archives of Sexual Behavior* 32 (2003): 537-544.

21. J. R. Meloy and M. J. Meloy, 'Autonomic Arousal in the Presence of Psychopathy: A Survey of Mental Health & Criminal Justice Professionals', *Journal of Threat Assessment* 2(2) (2003): 21-31.

22. J. J. Gunnell and S. J. Ceci, 'When Emotionality Trumps Reason: A Study of Individual Processing Style and Juror Bias', *Behavioural Sciences and the Law* 28(6) (2010): 850-877.

23. A. L. Glenn *et al.*, 'Early Temperamental and Psychophysiological Precursors of Adult Psychopathic Personality', *Journal of Abnormal Psychology* 116(3) (2007): 508-518.

24. From J. McCrone, 'Rebels With A Cause,' *New Scientist* 165 (2000): 22-27.

25. R. D. Hare, *Without Conscience*.

26. Maurice Chittenden, 'Trust me, telling fibs is sure sign of success', The Sunday Times, 16 May 2010.

27. Professor Russell Foster, neuroscientist at Oxford University, quoted in *The Times*, 14 January 2007.

28. J. Biederman, J. Newcorn and S. Sprich, 'Comorbidity of attention deficit hyperactivity disorder with conduct, depressive, anxiety, and other disorders', *American Journal of Psychiatry* 148(5) (1991): 564-577.

29. E. Colledge and R. J. R. Blair, 'Relationship between ADHD and psychopathic tendencies in children', *Personality and Individual Differences* 30 (2001): 1175-1187.

30. J. Peter and H Burbach, 'Neuropsychiatric connections of ADHD genes', *Lancet* 376 (October 2010): 1367-1368.

31. J. N. Geidd, J. Blumenthal, E. Molloy and F. X.

Castellanos, 'Brain imaging of attention deficit hyperactivity disorder', *Annals of New York Academy of Sciences* 931 (2001): 33-49.

32. James Blair, Derek Mitchell and Karina Blair, *The Psychopath: Emotion and the brain* (Wiley-Blackwell, 2005).

33. F. J. Zimmerman *et al.*, 'Early cognitive stimulation, emotional support and television watching as predictors of subsequent bullying among grade-school children', *Archives of Pediatrics & Adolescent Medicine* 159(4) (2005): 384-388.

34. J. B. Funk, 'Reevaluating the Impact of Video Games', *Clinical Pediatrics* 32(2) (1993): 86-90; quoted by Bernard Cesarone at http://ceep.crc.illinois.edu/ eecearchive/digests/1994/cesaro94.html (accessed 25 November 2010).

35. Youth TGI Survey, 2004.

36. Teresa Orange and Louise O'Flynn, *The Media Diet For Kids: A Parent's Survival Guide to TV & Computer Games* (Hay House, 2005).

37. 'The Final Report & Findings of the Safe School Initiative', 1 May 2002.

38. 'The Depressive and the Psychopath: The FBI's analysis of the Killers Motives', *Slate*, 20 April 2004.

39. Mary Ellen O'Toole, FBI, 'The School Shooter: A Threat Assessment Perspective', cited in www.fbi.gov.

40. E. Aronson, 'Reducing Hostility and Building Compassion: Lessons from the Jigsaw Classroom in *The Social Psychology of Good & Evil* (2004).

41. G. T. Harris, M. E. Rice and M. Lalumiere, 'Criminal Violence: The roles of psychopathy, neurodevelopmental insults and antisocial parenting', *Criminal Justice and Behaviour* 28 (2001): 402-426.

42. R. D. Hare, 'Psychopathy as a risk factor for

violence', *Psychiatric Quarterly* 70 (1999): 181-197.

43. R. D. Hare, *Without Conscience*, 168.

44. D. Stevens, T. Charman and R. J. R. Blair, 'Recognition of emotion in facial expressions and vocal tones in children with psychopathic tendencies', *Journal of Genetic Psychology*, 162(2) (2001): 201-211.

45. R. J. R. Blair and M. Coles, 'Expression recognition and behavioural problems in early adolescence', *Cognitive Development* 15 (2000): 421-434.

46. Based on K. Browne & M. Herbert, *Preventing Family Violence*, 1997.

47. Orville Gilbert Brim, *Look At Me! The Fame Motive From Childhood to Death* (University of Michigan Press, 2009).

48. Survey of 1032 16-year-olds carried out by www.intotheblue.com, reported in www.parentdish.co.uk, 19 February 2010.

49. Survey of 3000 British parents of pre-teens commissioned by *Let The Kids Loose*, Watch TV, reported by www.taylorherring.com, 6 October 2010.

50. Jib Fowles, professor of media studies at the University of Houston-Clear Lake and author of *Starstruck: Celebrity Performers and the American Public* (Prentice Hall, 1992).

51. Mark Young and Drew Pinsky, 'Narcissism and celebrity', *Journal of Research in Personality*, 40(5) (October 2006): 463-471.

52. David Wilson, 'Rigged and Grotesque, this puppet show is doomed', *Daily Mail*, 26 October 2010.

53. GirlGuides survey, 2008.

54. From the Association of Teachers and Lecturers (survey of primary and secondary teachers).

55. Richard Crew, 'The Ethics of Reality Television Producers', *Media Ethics* 18(2) (Spring 2007): 10, 19.

56. Oliver James, *Affluenza* (Vermilion, 2007).

57. R. D. Hare, L. N. McPherson & A. E. Forth, 'Male Psychopaths and their criminal careers,' *Journal of Consulting and Clinical Psychology*, 56 (1988): 710-14. Also, C. A. Cormier 'Psychopathy and Violent Recidivisim', *Law and Human Behaviour* 15(1991): 625-37

58. R. D. Hare, *Without Conscience*.

59. S. Baron-Cohen *et al.*, 'The amygdala theory of autism', *Neuroscience and Biobehavioral Reviews* 24 (2000): 355-364.

60. N. H. Kalin, 'The primate amygdala mediates acute fear but not the behavioral and physiological component of anxious temperament', *The Journal of Neuroscience* 21 (2001): 2067-74.

61. R. A. Richell *et al.*, 'Trust and Distrust: the perception of trustworthiness of faces in psychopathic and non-psychopathic offenders', *Personality & Individual Differences* 38(8) (2005): 1735-1744.

62. R. Adolphs, L. Sears and J. Piven, 'Abnormal processing of social information from faces in autism', *Journal of Cognitive Neuroscience* 13(2) (2001): 232-240.

63. H. Cleckley, *The Mask of Sanity* (5th en; St Louis, MO: Mosby, 1976).

64. D. T. Lykken, *The Antisocial Personalities* (Hillside, NJ: Lawrence Erlbaum Associates, Inc, 1995).

65. C. J. Patrick, 'Emotion and psychopathy: startling new insights', *Psychophysiology* 31 (1994): 319-330.

66. S. Arieti, 'Some elements of cognitive psychiatry', *American Journal of Psychotherapy* 21 (1967): 723-736.

67. S. S. Smith and J. P. Newman, 'Alcohol and drug abuse-dependence disorders in psychopathic and non-psychopathic criminal offenders', *Journal of Abnormal Psychology* 99 (1999): 430-439; J. F. Hemphill, S. D. Hart and R. D. Hare, 'Psychopathy and substance

use', *Journal of Personality Disorders* 8 (1994): 169-180.

68. K. Tourian *et al.*, 'Validity of three measures of antiso-
    ciality in predicting HIV risk behaviours in methadone-
    maintenance patients', *Drug and Alcohol Dependence* 47
    (1997): 99-107.

69. J. P. Newman *et al.*, 'Psychopathy and Psychopathology:
    Hare's Essential Contributions', in H. Herve and J. Yuille
    (eds) *Psychopathy in the Third Millennium: Theory and
    Research* (New York: Academic Press, 2003).

70. R. D. Hare, *Without Conscience.*

71. P. A. Arnett, S. S. Smith and J. P. Newman, 'Approach
    and avoidance motivation in psychopathic criminal
    offenders during passive avoidance', *Journal of Personality
    and Social Psychology* 72 (1997): 1413-1428.

72. R. D. Hare, 'Hare Psychopathy Checklist-Revised (PCL-
    R): 2nd Edition', *Technical Manual* (2003).